Walking Straight When Life Goes Sideways

Walking Straight When Life Goes Sideways

Essential Christian Truths for Enduring Life's Trials

CHRISTOPHER L. SCOTT

WIPF & STOCK · Eugene, Oregon

WALKING STRAIGHT WHEN LIFE GOES SIDEWAYS
Essential Christian Truths for Enduring Life's Trials

Wipf & Stock
An Imprint of Wipf and Stock Publishers
199 W. 8th Ave., Suite 3
Eugene, OR 97401

www.wipfandstock.com

PAPERBACK ISBN: 979-8-3852-4468-3
HARDCOVER ISBN: 979-8-3852-4469-0
EBOOK ISBN: 979-8-3852-4470-6

VERSION NUMBER 02/17/26

The article "The Persecution of Christians in the First Century" by Eckhard J. Schnabel (*Journal of the Evangelical Theological Society* 61 (2018) 525–47) is summarized with permission from the Evangelical Theological Society.

Dedicated to Jennifer and Luke

Contents

Preface

How did I get here? was the question I asked myself again and again. I was in room five of Samaritan Hospital with a heart and oxygen monitor attached to my finger; intravenous (IV) ports placed in both my arms; and a nasogastric (NG) tube inserted up my nose, down my throat, and into my stomach. Every thirty seconds the NG tube suctioned fluids out of my stomach and sent them to a bucket attached to the wall. Somehow my small intestine had twisted itself into a knot and no food or fluids could pass through it.

At this point in my life I was doing a job I loved and felt I had become good at it. Several days a week I was going for five-mile runs and felt good physically. Each morning I woke up early for a rich and satisfying quiet time with the Lord. At the age of thirty-eight I felt I was in the best spiritual, physical, and emotional shape of my life.

That morning in room five was the beginning of my seven-day stay in the hospital. During the first two days my NG tube prevented me from moving from my hospital bed unless a registered nurse unhooked me from the wall. During the first four days I was not allowed to eat or even have a sip of water. Eventually, through laparoscopic surgery and close monitoring of doctors and nurses, I was able to go home.

One week after being released from the hospital, on Christmas day, I found myself back in a hospital room, experiencing the same pain in my gut. While I was able to go home from the hospital that day, the next two years involved additional doctor visits, expensive MRIs, extreme pain, a colonoscopy, new food intolerances, and pain in my digestive system that I had never experienced before in my life.

You might be reading this asking the same question: *How did I get here?* You're in the middle of suffering and simply trying to figure out how to endure. Maybe you've been through suffering and are trying to reflect on what you experienced in order to make sense of it. Or maybe you have a friend or family member experiencing suffering and you're looking for a way to help him or her.

I present this book as a resource, not because I'm an expert on the *why* of suffering or the *how to* endure it, but as a fellow sufferer and a pastor hoping to share with you a few of my experiences along with expositions of Scripture related to suffering.

Whether you are someone enduring suffering right *now*, trying to *recover* from suffering, or trying to *help* someone through suffering, I pray this book comforts you and helps you. I look forward to our journey together as we discover from 1 Peter how to walk straight when life goes sideways.

Christopher L. Scott
Fall 2025

Acknowledgments

Special thanks to the team at Wipf and Stock for publishing this work. Everyone has been both kind and professional. It has been a privilege to work with you all.

I'm grateful to the men and women at Lakeview Missionary Church who first *heard* this material preached and hopefully have *seen* it lived out in their pastor.

A special thank-you to Pat O'Leary and Dennis Fountain for reading early versions of this book and for providing feedback.

Abbreviations

BDAG	Danker, Frederick W., Walter Bauer, William F. Arndt, and F. Wilbur Gingrich. *Greek-English Lexicon of the New Testament and Other Early Christian Literature.* 3rd ed. Chicago: University of Chicago Press, 2000
NASB	*NASB Study Bible.* Grand Rapids: Zondervan, 1999
NET	*NET Bible, Full Notes Edition.* Nashville: Thomas Nelson and Biblical Studies, 2019

1

First Things First

New relationships involve new responsibilities, requirements, and usually lead to new results. A new job means we must be on time, perform certain work, and as a result, get a specific amount of pay. Marrying a spouse requires we be faithful, kind, loving, and hopefully enjoy a life of fellowship together. Becoming a parent involves being responsible, being unselfish, getting to enjoy a relationship, and investing in another life. If we join a service club like Rotary or Lions or Kiwanis we are expected to give money, be a community ambassador, and help positive change occur in our community. If we become a citizen of a country we must obey laws and pay taxes, and then we enjoy the benefits of living in that country.

I want us first—before looking at suffering—to see what responsibilities and requirements are placed on followers of Jesus Christ. When we do this we'll see results from following him.

The first paragraph of 1 Peter answers questions we might have. The unbeliever might ask, "What will life look like if I become a Christian?" or "If I become a Christian, what is God going to do for me or to me?" The committed believer might ask, "I love Jesus, but how do I live out that love?" or "I read my Bible every day and pray throughout the day. How do I allow that to affect my life?" First Peter 1:1–12 is sometimes called a "Great Doxology" and it's theologically rich. It describes who we are as Christians and is a revelation of our great salvation. Peter explains how a relationship with Jesus Christ involves new requirements and produces new results in our lives.

RECIPIENTS

This letter begins with "Peter, an apostle of Jesus Christ" (1 Pet 1:1a). There is only one person in the New Testament with the name Peter. This was the same Peter that was personally called (Matt 10:1–4) and commissioned by Christ (John 20:19–23). Peter spent three years with Jesus Christ and another thirty years as an apostle leading the church. The church was built on his teaching (Acts 2:42; Eph 2:20).

The readers of Peter's letter are "those who reside as aliens, scattered throughout Pontus, Galatia, Cappadocia, Asia, and Bithynia" (1 Pet 1:1b). The term *alien* means sojourners, exiles, or foreign residents.[1] The readers are aliens because they are temporary residents on earth while their eternal citizenship is in heaven.

The places Pontus, Galatia, Cappadocia, Asia, and Bithynia were provinces of Asia Minor, north of the Taurus Mountains, in modern-day Turkey. Peter is addressing the believers that live in these five provinces.[2]

Peter writes to people "chosen according to the foreknowledge of God the Father, by the sanctifying work of the Spirit, to obey Jesus Christ and be sprinkled with His blood" (1 Pet 1:1c–2). Peter describes these readers as those who are "chosen," which reveals a sense in Scripture that God knows us and selects us to be part of his family. The nation of Israel was often described by God as his chosen and elect people.[3]

1. Ryrie, *Study Bible*, 1543.

2. For additional background on suffering addressed in 1 Peter, see Scott, "Suffering in 1 Peter."

3. See Exod 19:3–6; Deut 4:37; 7:6–8; 10:15; 14:2; Ps 106:5; Isa 14:1; 41:8–18; 43:20; 45:4; 51:2; 65:9, 15, 23.

There are two categories of thought as it relates to what it means to be chosen by God. The Arminian or Wesleyan would say, "God chose me because God knew I would choose him." The Calvinist would say, "I chose God because God chose me." Admittedly, it's hard to describe which view is correct from this verse. If we focus on the two words *chosen* and *foreknown*, I think we might lean toward the Calvinist interpretation. For the sake of this work, as it relates to suffering, we are going to assume the Calvinist position. I believe the broad teaching of Scripture is that God knows us and selects us to be part of his family.

Peter next goes deeper into what it means to be chosen by God. Peter transitions from directly addressing the recipients of his letter to the regeneration that has occurred inside of them.

REGENERATION

First Peter 1:3–5 describes our source of hope and is part of a larger section (1 Pet 1:3—2:10)[4] where Peter counts the blessings of God's redeemed children.[5] The word *regeneration* is the word we use to describe God's "supernatural act of imparting life."[6] This work of God happens the moment we place our faith in God.[7]

As Peter describes our regeneration he says that God pardons us: "Blessed be the God and Father of our Lord Jesus Christ, who according to His great mercy has caused us to be born again to a living hope through the resurrection of Jesus Christ from the dead" (1 Pet 1:3). The phrase "His great mercy" means we've been saved because of our faith in God. This gives us "a living hope." We have this great expectation because of what Jesus Christ did.

4. Here's my outline of 1 Peter: introduction (1:1–2), life in the Son (1:3—2:10), life in society (2:11—3:12), life in suffering (3:13—4:19), life in service (5:1–11), and conclusion (5:12–14).

5. Some believe 1 Pet 1:3–12 might have been adapted from a hymn. Keener, *1 Peter*, 63n1.

6. Ryrie, *Survey of Bible Doctrine*, 76.

7. Ryrie, *Survey of Bible Doctrine*, 76.

As Peter describes our regeneration he says that God preserves our inheritance: "To obtain an inheritance which is imperishable and undefiled and will not fade away, reserved in heaven for you" (1 Pet 1:4). In this verse Peter uses three adjectives each starting with the same Greek letter (alpha). First-century writers sometimes used this device (known as alliteration) to make their words catchy and pleasing to the ears. Those words are *aphtharton* which is translated as "imperishable," *amianton* which is translated as "undefiled," and *amaranton* which is translated as "will not fade away." Those three adjectives describe how our inheritance is "reserved in heaven." That word for "reserved" is in the perfect tense in Greek, which indicates that our inheritance has been put in safe keeping, it can't change, and it's permanent.[8] Peter is telling us that our inheritance won't spoil like fruit, and it won't fade like paint.

As Peter describes our regeneration he says that God protects our salvation: "Who are protected by the power of God through faith for a salvation ready to be revealed in the last time" (1 Pet 1:5). This verse is a great place to pause and review how different authors of Scripture sometimes use the same words in different ways. Let's use the metaphor of a boat to illustrate how Paul, James, and Peter each use *salvation* in a different way. Paul's use of salvation is for initiation. He looks at salvation as how you get into the boat: where it's located and what steps must be taken to get into it. James's use of salvation is progressive. He looks at salvation as what you do when you're in the boat: rowing, removing water from the bottom, adjusting the sails. Peter's use of salvation is glorification. He looks at salvation as a future experience to look forward to eternally in heaven: the ultimate destination in which the boat will arrive. This was Peter's way of saying salvation is a living hope because it's part of our future and is an expectation we possess.[9]

Peter's three verses about our regeneration cause us to realize that *what we have can't be taken away*. Our eternal inheritance—based on our faith in God—is in a lockbox and only God has the key. This is important because if God gave it, then we can't lose it.

8. Wallace, *Greek Grammar*, 573.

9. Keener, *1 Peter*, 71.

If our salvation and our inheritance were based on something we have done, then there's the possibility that we might do something to lose it. But since there's nothing we did to gain salvation, there is nothing we can do to lose our salvation. It's similar to the layaway department that stores like Walmart used to have. You took things there, paid for them as you wanted, and when you were ready to pick them up, you went and got them. After you had paid for the items you could even leave them there for up to thirty days. (That was a nice convenience if you had snoopy little kids always scouring the house for their presents.) Our inheritance as a follower of Jesus Christ is on layaway in heaven. It's been paid for by the blood of Christ. It's waiting for us and nothing can ruin it. This security of our inheritance is important because next Peter talks about suffering.

REJOICING

Peter continues this introductory paragraph by writing, "In this you greatly rejoice, even though now for a little while, if necessary, you have been distressed by various trials, so that the proof of your faith, being more precious than gold which is perishable, even though tested by fire, may be found to result in praise and glory and honor at the revelation of Jesus Christ; and though you have not seen Him, you love Him, and though you do not see Him now, but believe in Him, you greatly rejoice with joy inexpressible and full of glory, obtaining as the outcome of your faith the salvation of your souls" (1 Pet 1:6–9).

These verses describe our attitude of hope. Peter introduces this theme of suffering—that's woven throughout the book—in verse 6 when he writes that these people are "distressed by various trials." In this letter Peter uses the word *suffer* fourteen times. As he describes the difficulties of these Christians, he also uses the words *trials, slandered, reviled, harshly treated, fiery ordeal,* and *testing.* He gives us four reasons to rejoice in suffering.

Peter tells his readers to rejoice in sufferings because they are temporary, "now for a little while" (1 Pet 1:6). In other words, suffering hurts now, but in light of eternity, it's temporary. It's easier to endure suffering when we learn it won't last forever.[10]

Peter tells his readers to rejoice in sufferings because they are testing: "So that the proof of your faith, being more precious than gold which is perishable, even though tested by fire, may be found to result in praise and glory and honor at the revelation of Jesus Christ" (1 Pet 1:7). Trials do to faith what fire does to gold: they purge and purify it. Notice the purpose phrase there, "so that." Those trials are deemed necessary by God to purge things from our lives and purify our faith. Specifically, trials purify our faith because they reveal the inadequacy of everything else in our lives. We learn to trust God in every situation through trials. When someone says, "God loves you and has a wonderful plan for your life," I always want to raise my hand and say, "There are footnotes to that statement that you're not sharing." One of those footnotes is this: God allows us to experience trials, sufferings, and testings. Examples of this are when Jacob tells his brothers that their actions were done in evil, but God meant it for good (Gen 50:20) and when Paul tells the believers in Rome that God works all things for good according to his plans for those who love him (Rom 8:28). The late R. C. Sproul wrote, "God's hand is in earthly trials that are unjustly foisted upon us by wicked people. The hand of God trumps the evil intent of those who wound us, and He uses, in His gracious providence, those various experiences of affliction and pain for His glory and for our ultimate edification."[11] We, as believers in Jesus Christ, rejoice in those sufferings (even though it's hard) because we know they are testings used by God for our own good (even though we don't yet know why).

Peter tells his readers to rejoice in sufferings because they are tangible: "And though you have not seen Him, you love Him, and though you do not see Him now, but believe in Him, you greatly rejoice with joy inexpressible and full of glory" (1 Pet 1:8). The focus of our faith as Christians is not abstract knowledge, but instead is the person of Jesus Christ. This was perhaps easier for

10. Keener, *1 Peter*, 73.

11. Sproul, *1–2 Peter*, 35.

Peter because he physically walked and talked with Jesus. We do not have that same privilege. Pastor Tony Evans says, "All trials are designed to do three things: prove your faith, develop your faith, and glorify your Savior. You never know what you believe until you face a test. The heavenly goldsmith wants to refine your character."[12]

Peter tells his readers to rejoice in sufferings because they are total: "Obtaining as the outcome of your faith the salvation of your souls" (1 Pet 1:9). This verse tells us about the completion of our salvation. As believers in Christ we are temporarily delivered from the power of sin in our lives now, even though we are still tempted to sin. We will experience a future life in heaven when sin will no longer be a temptation. The result of our faith is a constant deliverance from the power of sin, yet when we receive our eternal glory in heaven we will experience ultimate deliverance from sin.[13]

As we read these verses it's important we realize that *what we have as Christians helps us endure suffering*. The British preacher of twentieth-century England, Dr. Martin Lloyd Jones, wrote, "The Christian is not one who has become immune to what is happening round and about him."[14] We as Christians cannot blissfully act like we live in Wonderland and are immune to the world. We are not Mr. Magoo who escapes terrible situations through haphazard luck. The Christian life does not exempt a believer from experiencing affliction. In fact, as we read Peter's words, we will expect affliction because we are Christians.

When we endure suffering we get stronger. Someone in our church recently broke her pelvis while hiking. While the ordeal caused her extreme pain, the doctors told her that her break was not as bad as it could have been. The break was not straight, but instead curved because as her bone broke, it encountered a stronger spot, which redirected the break. If the break had been straight, she would have needed surgery, and had a more difficult recovery. But she avoided surgery and has made a full recovery

12. Evans, *Evans Bible Commentary*, 1351.

13. MacArthur, *MacArthur Study Bible*, 1679.

14. Jones, *Spiritual Depression*, 220.

because of that stronger location in her pelvis. That stronger spot was the location where a surgeon had drilled into her pelvis in the process of replacing her hip just a few years earlier. The spot where they drilled was damaged—of course—but when our bones are broken there is a short period of time in which the bone grows back stronger than it was before.[15]

Suffering makes us stronger and helps us withstand future problems. As a pastor I can honestly say that some of the holiest people I know are Christians who have endured the most suffering. Did they endure suffering because they were holy? Or are they holy because they endured suffering? I would say they are holy because of their suffering.

I think Peter—if I can enter his mind—starts this letter reminding us that we are chosen and foreknown by God so that we realize we are never outside of God's plan, even if we are in pain or suffering. It's hard to write, but enduring pain and suffering might be part of God's plan and will for our lives.

These precious words we have from Peter should be held in the highest esteem. He was one of the few men that walked with Jesus, ate with Jesus, talked with Jesus, and saw Jesus answer people's questions. When Peter wrote this letter he had thirty years to reflect on who Jesus was and how Christians should live. Peter wrote this letter to aliens—citizens of heaven temporarily living in Asia Minor—and he's writing to you and me who are citizens of heaven temporarily living on earth now. He starts with things of first importance: what we have can't be taken away and what we have helps us endure suffering. Let's continue this journey together and discover what Peter teaches about how to endure suffering.

Now that we have a proper understanding of our identity in Christ, we can correctly interpret what suffering looks like for us. Next we'll learn what type of suffering Christians endure as well as how to endure that suffering.

15. McVean, "Broken Bones Grow Stronger," para. 2.

2

Sharing the Savior in Suffering

"No good deed goes unpunished." I'm sure you've heard that before. It's a phrase we often say when someone encounters bad because of the good they did.

In America we have a law that protects the "good doer" called the "Good Samaritan law." Under the protection of this law, if you help someone in danger, you cannot be sued by the person for any harm you might cause to him in saving him from greater harm. For example, if I pull you from a burning car to save your life but break your pinky finger, you can't sue me for that.

When Christians do good, do we expect protection from harm and suffering? If we go to church, read our Bibles, pray every day, attend Bible study groups, faithfully give, regularly serve in outreach, and visit the sick in hospitals, then will we be exempt from suffering? Is suffering God's punishment to us because we have not done enough good works to please him? Is suffering just a matter of us being in the wrong place at the wrong time?

In this book I want to take you through 1 Pet 3:13—4:19, which helps believers endure suffering. In 1 Pet 3:13–17, Peter tells us that authentic Christians are slandered and will experience suffering, but that slandering and suffering give Christians an opportunity to share about their hope as Christians. In other words, our hope in Christ leads to our witness for Christ. In these five verses we'll see three instructions for what we are supposed to do when we encounter suffering.

PRINCIPLES IN SUFFERING

The general principle in suffering Peter explains is this: "Who is there to harm you if you prove zealous for what is good?" (1 Pet 3:13). What Peter is saying here is that you usually don't suffer for doing good.[1] But there is an exception to the principle. "But even if you should suffer for the sake of righteousness, you are blessed. And do not fear their intimidation, and do not be troubled" (1 Pet 3:14). Here we get the answer to the question of the previous verse: What do I do if I suffer even after doing good? First Peter 3:14 reveals three truths that Christians must recognize.

First, we learn what might happen: "But even if you should suffer for the sake of righteousness." This phrase is a fourth-class conditional statement in Greek. In English we know of conditional statements as "If . . . then . . ." Conditional statements have a protasis ("if" condition) and an apodosis ("then" consequent). In Greek there are four types of conditional statements. The fourth-class conditional statement describes something as possible, but improbable. It's a way to describe a possible condition in the future, but a remote possibility. It's like saying, "If perhaps this should occur."[2] Peter implies that this type of suffering was not normal, but could happen and might have happened to some of the readers (see 1 Pet 4:4, 12–19). In other words, suffering when doing good is rare.

Second, we learn what will happen: "You are blessed." This is the "then" part of the fourth-class conditional statement. The apodosis ("then" consequent) is a blessing. This is interesting because it's not what we expect. When suffering happens we intuitively ask,

1. Earlier in this letter Peter taught that if you submit to the government (1 Pet 2:13–17), submit to bosses (1 Pet 2:18–25), submit to your spouse (1 Pet 3:1–7), and submit to each other (1 Pet 3:8–12), then people are not usually harmed for acts of kindness.

2. Wallace, *Greek Grammar*, 699–701.

"What did I do wrong?" or "Where was the misstep I had?" We ask these questions because we think there's a mistake we made somewhere along the way. Yet we are taught something different here: the sufferers are blessed because God uses suffering from good works as part of his plan. Suffering, in this context, is not seen as a sign we are outside of God's plan; instead, suffering is a sign we are in God's will and plan.[3]

Third, we learn how to handle it: "And do not fear their intimidation, and do not be troubled." This is a quote of Isa 8:12–13. God speaks to the prophet Isaiah about the king of Assyria coming to Judah (Isa 8:6–10). In that message God tells Isaiah to tell the people of Judah not to fear Assyria, but instead to fear God.[4]

Peter's first instruction for us in suffering is that *we need to be fearful of God.* It's easy to be scared by the various economic troubles, pandemic diseases, and environmental problems. But we need to remember that we fear God, not man, and we need to believe in God's sovereignty more than our earthly circumstances.

It shouldn't matter what man may do to us, but what matters is what God may do through us. When our boss asks us to commit to working every single Sunday we say, "I worship God with my family on Sundays." When a friend in school has drugs and he wants us to do drugs with him, we decline because we know it's wrong and dangerous. When coworkers ignore safety rules because they can get their work done faster, we follow the safety rules even if it makes our coworkers look irresponsible. When a family member has a specific political opinion and it's contrary to Scripture, we gently and gracefully say we disagree even though we know it will cause friction.

Stanley Toussaint was a young Christian man working in a hardware store doing various jobs. He worked hard and tried to do his work with integrity. One week the shipping clerk went on

3. Swindoll, *Insights on 1 & 2 Peter*, 215.

4. Another interpretation of this message to Isaiah is that God was preparing Isaiah for a ministry where the people reject Isaiah's teachings and that God would sustain Isaiah through it. Either interpretation reveals how to handle future suffering.

vacation so Stanley was asked to do the man's job for that week. However, Stanley was able to do all of the shipping clerk's work in one hour each morning, then went on and did other miscellaneous jobs throughout the day. When the shipping clerk returned, the store manager was upset with the shipping clerk because a young man was able to do the shipping clerk's work in one hour while the shipping clerk took eight hours to do the same amount of work every day. As a result, that shipping clerk was very rude to Stanley.[5] But that's one example of how we fear God, not man. It's a reminder to focus on God's opinion of us, not what humans think about us.

Pastor and writer Warren Wiersbe has rightly said, "Our enemies might *hurt* us, but they cannot *harm* us. Only we can harm ourselves if we fail to trust God."[6] When faced with difficult situations we face our fears with God by our side.

In 1 Pet 3:13–14 we learned about a general principle in suffering. Next Peter moves on to tell us what to do with this general principle.

PRACTICES IN SUFFERING

The "but" that begins the next two verses shows us a contrast that starts with our conduct: "But sanctify Christ as Lord in your hearts, always being ready to make a defense to everyone who asks you to give an account for the hope that is in you, yet with gentleness and reverence" (1 Pet 3:15).

Conduct

As Peter describes our conduct he first labels our inward dedication: "Sanctify Christ as Lord in your hearts." Contrary to the fear of others, we place Christ at the center of our lives and at the center of our hearts. To sanctify Christ means to turn everything over to

5. Toussaint, "Subjection."
6. Wiersbe, *Be Hopeful*, 96.

him, to live only to please him, and to glorify him. It means we are setting him in a unique place as Lord and master over our lives.

Next Peter describes our conduct in relation to our outward action: "Always being ready to make a defense to everyone who asks you to give an account for the hope that is in you, yet with gentleness and reverence." This outward action includes timing—"always being ready" (v. 15b). This is something we can share informally when needed. We don't need a piece of paper nor do we need to Google our answers.

The outward action also includes a task: "To make a defense to everyone who asks you to give an account for the hope that is in you." The word "defense" here is the Greek noun *apologian* and comes from the verb *apologeomai*, which means "to answer back" or "a defense."[7] A literal way to translate it would be, "ready for an answer" (as Paul used it in Acts 22:1 and Phil 1:7, 16).[8] Our word for apologetics comes from those words. But what do we defend? In this context, it appears to be our future hope in spite of our present suffering: "The hope that is in you." The curious person might not specifically ask about our hope, but because our hope is the source of everything we do—since Christ is consecrated in our hearts—our answers naturally stem from our hope.

The outward action also includes a tool: "Yet with gentleness and reverence." The late R. C. Sproul has wisely said, "When we engage in debates and arguments, we sometimes allow ourselves to be overcome with the heat of the moment and generate more heat than light."[9] As Christians we show gentleness as we outwardly describe our hope.

Conscience

While 1 Pet 3:15 tells us about our conduct, 1 Pet 3:16 tells us about our conscience: "And keep a good conscience so that in the thing

7. BDAG, s.v. "apologeomai."
8. Robertson, *Word Pictures*, "1 Pet 3:15."
9. Sproul, *1–2 Peter*, 124.

in which you are slandered, those who revile your good behavior in Christ will be put to shame." When I hear the word *conscience* I'm reminded of a little girl that once defined conscience this way: "Something that makes you tell your mother what you did before your brother or sister does."[10] But honestly, the conscience is what occurs in us from our sin by producing guilt, shame, and doubt. While we might act out sin and do evil now, our conscious convicts us of our wrong later.

When we live a life free of ongoing and unconfessed sin and follow the commands of God, we enjoy a good conscience because we know the suffering was not caused by us. When we act righteously in the midst of unjust suffering it puts others to shame, not us. When other people slander us and do bad things to us yet we still have a kind and loving attitude, it puts others in a bad light.

Peter's second instruction for us in suffering is *we need to be fervent to defend God.* This is not the responsibility of scholars, PhDs, or just pastors. We all are responsible to have a ready defense and an explanation of our hope in God.

But a defense of what? It should be a defense of our faith in hopeless situations and thus in suffering. The late pastor and writer Warren Wiersbe once stated, "A crisis creates the opportunity for witness when a believer behaves with faith and hope, because the unbelievers will then sit up and take notice."[11] In our times of suffering our witness speaks the loudest. In our suffering our words weigh the most. Many times people have told me, "Pastor, your words mean more now because I know that you understand what suffering is." I've also heard, "When you pray for me I know it's important because I know you don't feel well." Because our words, when spoken during suffering, have greater impact we must be ready to explain what we believe and why we believe it.

I like the interaction between Joe and Bill about the doctrine of Bill's church. Joe asks Bill, "What do you believe about God?" Bill responds, "I believe what my church believes." So Joe asks, "What does your church believe?" Bill responds, "My church

10. Bramer, *Bible Reader's Joke Book*, 445.

11. Wiersbe, *Be Hopeful*, 96.

believes what I believe." Joe presses Bill further and asks, "What do you and your church believe?" Bill smiles and responds, "We both believe the same thing."[12]

When we encounter suffering we need to be ready to explain our faith in God to others. We need to know what we believe and why we believe it. Pastor John MacArthur has written, "The believer must understand what he believes and why one is a Christian, and then be able to articulate one's beliefs humbly, thoughtfully, and biblically."[13] When we articulate our beliefs it means we provide deep answers, not surfacy platitudes we see on bumper stickers or hear in thirty-second Christian radio devotions.

This means we need to know the basic beliefs and practices of the Christian life. We need to know why we follow the direction of the sixty-six books in the Bible and not the Book of Mormon. We need to know why we accept a variety of translations but not the New World translation that Jehovah's Witnesses use. We need to know why eternal life is only offered through Jesus Christ. We need to know how salvation is based on faith, not good behavior. We might not be able to argue someone into becoming a Christian, but we need to know enough for them to respect us because we know what we believe.

In addition to Peter's teaching on principles and practices in suffering, he also wants to add one little piece of information onto what he's already shared.

POTENTIAL IN SUFFERING

In verse 17 we come across another one of those fourth-class conditional statements sometimes found in Greek. (Remember a fourth-class condition in Greek is possible, but improbable.) Peter writes, "For it is better, if God should will it so, that you suffer for doing what is right rather than for doing what is wrong" (1 Pet 3:17).

12. Bramer, *Bible Reader's Joke Book*, 445.

13. MacArthur, *MacArthur Study Bible*, 1914.

Three of the five words in the phrase "God should will it so" begin with the same Greek letter. It's the Greek letter *theta* that makes the sound of *th* in *thing* in English.[14] The phrase is *theloi to thelēma tou theou*. First-century writers and orators sometimes used sounds in language to highlight certain features of what they were communicating. Here Peter is emphasizing God's will might be for us to suffer.

The text could literally be translated, "If the will of God should so will it." The idea is this: suffering for doing good is not what God normally wills, even though it does happen. But it may have happened to some of the readers.[15]

Peter's third instruction for us in suffering is *we need to be faithful to God's will*. It's hard to write this but suffering for doing good may be God's will. Peter will write in the next chapter, "Therefore, those also who suffer according to the will of God shall entrust their souls to a faithful Creator in doing what is right" (1 Pet 4:19). Let's use my experience as an example. What if God wanted me to endure a seven-day hospital stay and years of digestive struggles as part of his will for me? What if it was God's intention to put me through suffering so that my ministry as a pastor would mean more to my congregation? What if it was for the benefit of others in my church that God made me endure suffering? When we commit to follow God with our lives and confess him as Lord, it means we go where he leads regardless if we like it or not. It also means we follow him even if we are unsure of where we are going.

For almost two decades I've traveled to Alaska each year to spend time with my family who live there. Many of those winter trips included riding snow mobiles following my dad. Sometimes we would start a ride going to a specific place, but after we began our trip he would decide to go somewhere different. I would follow his snow tracks wherever he went. I didn't know where we were going, I didn't know how to get home, but I was relying on him to take me someplace safe.

14. Mounce, *Basics of Biblical Greek*, 8.

15. *NET*, 2312.

Following our heavenly Father is similar to that. We follow God every day, we follow God in every direction, and we follow God in every decision. When we follow God we don't "take time off" from God or say, "I don't like that God, today you're on your own." We follow him regardless of what might happen or where he might take us, even if it includes suffering. We do this because we trust God knows what he is doing, that he will protect us, and that he has a plan for us.

Suffering does happen, even to Christians. Peter's first thought on suffering is to kindly instruct these readers that suffering might come even if they have done lots of good. In other words, it's as if Peter is saying, "Even if you do all the good that I just told you about, you might suffer because of it."

So if you're a Christian and you're suffering don't feel guilty, don't be confused, and try not to get discouraged. Instead, keep a good conscience and keep doing good. Use that suffering as an opportunity to tell others about the hope that you have in Christ. That's the topic of our next chapter together in which we will learn what suffering does in us and how we describe our hope in Christ to others.

3

Trial by Water

GEORGIANNA WORKED IN New York City as a nurse in a hospital. She and her husband Ted were both faithful members of their church and had three beautiful kids. The youngest of their children was an eleven-month-old girl named Jane. Georgianna was a good mom dedicated to her children. One evening, Georgianna and her family were having dinner when their eleven-month-old leaned back in her high-chair, fell, and hit the back of her head on the floor.

After a lot of crying and some consoling from mom and dad, she eventually settled down. Since Georgianna was a nurse and her husband Ted also worked in the medical field, they determined they didn't need to go to the emergency room. They thought their daughter was okay. They both knew Jane had her one-year check-up in just a couple of days, so they decided to tell the doctor at that appointment and make sure everything was okay.

When they went to see their doctor they told the doctor about the accident in which Jane fell out of her chair. The doctor decided to have an x-ray and CT scan done. The x-ray showed a small crack in the baby's skull, but the CT scan showed no other injuries. The doctor told Georgianna the crack would heal like most bones do.

One week later Georgianna was surprised when police detectives and Child Protective Service (CPS) workers showed up at her house to take away her one-year-old daughter and her other two children. Someone had reported to CPS that child abuse was occurring in their home!

Georgianna and Ted worked for nine months to get their kids back. Since Georgianna was a nurse in a hospital that sometimes worked with kids, she was unable to perform her job while this case was in process. Georgianna and Ted endured nine months of difficulties, shame, and a criminal charge.[1]

I share that story—and I will finish it at the end of the chapter—as a way to remind you that sometimes suffering occurs in our lives unjustly. Sometimes we endure suffering that we didn't cause and we didn't deserve. Generally, people are not harmed for acts of kindness, but sometimes they are. Suffering comes even when we're doing the right things. Knowing that unjust suffering sometimes occurs gives us permission to honestly ask: Is there a model for us to follow when it comes to unjust suffering? How do we talk about God to people that cause our suffering? Is there a way we can prepare for suffering? Do we have confidence God will bring us through it?

The passage I want us to base our discussion on is 1 Pet 3:18–22. These five verses are in the middle of a paragraph (1 Pet 3:13—4:6) that continue Peter's thoughts he began in 3:13–17 about unjust suffering. In 1 Pet 3:18–22 we'll learn about the four characteristics of Christian suffering.

As we begin I want to assure you this paragraph is as difficult to interpret as it is to apply, so let me summarize it: suffering occurs in our lives just like Christ experienced suffering, so we need to expect it, prepare for it, proclaim Christ in it, and trust we will experience ultimate vindication from it. We will learn from these five verses that the ultimate sacrifice by the ultimate Savior leads to the ultimate salvation.

1. Keller, *Walking with God*, 125–29.

CHRIST'S SUFFERING

Peter describes Christ's suffering this way: "For Christ also died for sins once for all, the just for the unjust, so that He might bring us to God, having been put to death in the flesh, but made alive in the spirit" (1 Pet 3:18). There are four essential elements to Christ's suffering we need to draw out of this verse.

First, Christ's suffering was singular: "Christ also died for sins once for all." Notice that phrase is past tense. This was a single event. Under the old covenant in the Old Testament, Jews offered multiple sacrifices, then repeated the process the next year at Passover. Under the new covenant in the New Testament Christ offered a one-time sacrifice. It was a one-time perpetual sacrifice and no other sacrifices are needed (see Heb 9:26–28).

Second, Christ's suffering was sufficient: "once for all" emphasizes that Christ's work was enough. His sacrifice was complete and sufficient to pay for our sins. It was his gift and didn't require human effort from us.

Third, Christ's suffering was a substitution: "the just for the unjust" describes the sinlessness of our Savior. Jesus was fully God and fully human, yet he never sinned. He never sinned and therefore could take the place of sinners in order to satisfy God's wrath against sin (2 Cor 5:21).

Perhaps the best way to explain Christ as the perfect man taking our place is in the form of a story. A high school teacher needed to take a day off so a substitute teacher was placed in her classroom that day. That substitute had never missed a day of work, always completed the lesson plans for the classes she worked in, and the kids all behaved well while under her teaching. But on this day the school principal was told that she must fire one staff member that day in order to meet the payroll budget for the year. In order to make it fair the principal decided to randomly select a classroom and fire the teacher that happened to be in that classroom.[2] So the principal randomly selected a classroom and it

2. I know Jesus was not a random selection by God the Father, so let's not take the metaphor too far.

was the class in which the perfect substitute teacher happened to be working in that day. The next day the regular teacher for that class realized what happened: she should have been let go, but the substitute teacher took her place! Now imagine that was Christ taking our place. You and I should have been crucified on a cross for our sins, yet Jesus took our place.

Fourth, Christ's suffering was successful: "So that He might bring us to God." This phrase is part of a purpose clause in Greek starting with the particle *hina*. The verb used there, *prosagagē*, means "to lead or bring to (Matt 18:24), to approach (Eph 2:18), to present us to God on the basis of his atoning death for us, which has opened the way (Rom 3:25; Heb 10:19f)."[3]

The first characteristic Peter teaches us about suffering is that *we experience unrighteous suffering just like Christ did.* Let's reread 1 Pet 3:17 to give us the proper context of Christ's suffering described in 1 Pet 3:18. "For it is better, if God should will it so, that you suffer for doing what is right rather than for doing what is wrong." In the last chapter, Peter taught that suffering might happen to us even if we do good works. According to Peter, if you submit to government (1 Pet 2:13–17), submit to bosses at work (1 Pet 2:18–25), submit to your spouse (1 Pet 3:1–7), and submit to each other (1 Pet 3:8–12), then you still might suffer.

Peter again reminds us that believers might encounter suffering just as Christ suffered unjustly at the hand of God. It's hard to write that believers will experience unjust suffering. But, if Jesus was a perfect person and was killed like a criminal, should we as imperfect people expect to experience anything different?

An example of this is the persecution that people received when Martin Luther began to speak out against the unbiblical actions of the Roman Catholic Church in the sixteenth century. He wanted to restore the Catholic Church back to what Scripture taught. It was never his desire to start a new Christian church. So he wrote books and pamphlets that were critical of the unbiblical practices of the Roman Catholic Church. As you can imagine, the Roman Catholic Church was upset and organized public gatherings

3. Robertson, *Word Pictures*, "1 Pet 3:18."

to collect and burn Luther's books. However, those gatherings started to target Luther's followers. The persecution became so severe that on July 1, 1523, two men who were followers of Luther's teaching were added to the bonfire of books! Later, several printers would pay with their lives simply for reproducing Protestant texts.[4] While that story is almost unfathomable, it should not surprise Christians that we experience unjust suffering just as Christ did.

While we have learned about Christ's suffering, what did Christ do during that suffering? Peter tells us that next.

CHRIST'S SHARING

First Peter 3:18 taught us Jesus was made alive in spirit. Meaning, while his physical body was dead he was still alive spiritually. His true inner life—his own spirit[5]—was still alive and active even when his physical body was killed. His flesh (humanness) was dead but his spirit (deity) was alive (see Luke 23:46).

The Message

With that stated, next Peter tells us that Jesus had a message, "in which also He went and made proclamation to the spirits now in prison" (1 Pet 3:19a). Because Jesus was still alive in spirit he went and did work. He had a message to share, "He went and made a proclamation." In spite of his death he had triumphed and was victorious. The Greek word for "proclamation" here is *ekēryxen* (from *kēryssō*), which means to make a public declaration,[6] but not a "preaching invitation" because that Greek word is *euangelizō*.[7]

4. Pettegree and Weduwen, *Library*, 114.

5. The Greek word used there is *pneumati*, from *pneuma*. The best English-Greek lexicon, BDAG, explains, "Evidently in ref. to the manner of Jesus' movement; *pneuma* is that part of Christ which, in contrast to *sarx*, did not pass away in death, but survived as an individual entity after death." BDAG, s.v. "pneuma."

6. BDAG, s.v. "kēryssō."

7. Every occurrence of this Greek verb in the New Testament describes the

But where did Jesus go and to whom did Jesus preach?[8] Jesus went to Hades and declared victory to the souls there. I believe his proclamation to the souls in Hades was this: "I've conquered death. The grave couldn't hold me."

The Audience

While Jesus had a message, Peter also tells us Jesus had an audience: "To the spirits now in prison, who once were disobedient, when the patience of God kept waiting in the days of Noah, during the construction of the ark, in which a few, that is, eight persons, were brought safely through the water" (1 Pet 3:19b–20). Like I shared earlier, 1 Pet 3:19–21 are some of the most difficult verses in the entire Bible to translate, interpret, and to apply.

Who are these spirits that Jesus went and proclaimed victory to after his death? There are several interpretations, but the one I hold is that during Christ's three days in the grave, he went to Hades and proclaimed victory over all the disobedient, unrepentant, and nonbelieving souls there. The enemies of Noah are used by Peter as an example of all the souls—perhaps the most severe example—of people that rejected God.

The second characteristic Peter teaches us about suffering is that *as Christians we proclaim victory over those who insult, ridicule, and cause us suffering*. Peter mentions Noah in this passage as an example of someone who was uniquely called by God and who lived in a difficult time. Noah was a man of outstanding faith among his generation and kept doing the will of God even when he appeared a failure. Noah was mocked and ridiculed because of his obedience to God.

---

gospel being preached except for 1 Thess 3:6 and Rev 10:7.

8. The New Testament teaches us—specifically Luke 16:19–31—that when Jesus died he temporarily went to Hades/Sheol. In Luke 23:43 Jesus went to paradise immediately at death. Paradise and Abraham's bosom are a part of Sheol/Hades. Acts 2:27, 31 says Jesus was not abandoned or left in Hades, implying he went there. Ephesians 4:8–10 says that during Jesus's three days of death he went there, got the Old Testament saints that were saved by faith, and he took them to heaven.

If my interpretation is correct, then Christ went and proclaimed victory during his apparent time of suffering! We, too, preach to those who insult us and ridicule us. When other people cause our suffering we proclaim our faith in Christ in the face of the suffering they give us. It's like telling people that nothing they say or do will change us. "Even though you have harmed me, I still love you and care for you." Another might be, "Even though you say mean things to me, I still will be nice to you." Or "Even though you took my idea and presented it as your own in that meeting, I still help you when you need help."

From here we transition from what Jesus did during his death to what he accomplished for us in his resurrection.

CHRIST'S SUSTAINING

We are not done with the hard parts of this passage yet. Let's look at the next verse: "Corresponding to that, baptism now saves you—not the removal of dirt from the flesh, but an appeal to God for a good conscience—through the resurrection of Jesus Christ" (1 Pet 3:21). At the beginning of the verse we read, "Corresponding to that," which refers to how Noah and seven other persons were brought safely through the flood. This is Peter's way of saying that just as that ark was a way God saved them, we, too, experience a way God saves us—not with water, but a spiritual resurrection.

Let's clarify a few points. The ark did not literally save Noah, God did. The water for our baptism did not literally save us, God did. When we read "baptism" by water, we should view it as that outward symbol of an inward change that has occurred.

For example, 1 Cor 12:13 tells us, "For by one Spirit we were all baptized into one body, whether Jews or Greeks, whether slaves or free, and we were all made to drink of one Spirit." And in Rom 6:2–4 we learn, "Do you not know that all of us who have been baptized into Christ Jesus have been baptized into His death? Therefore we have been buried with Him through baptism into death, so that as Christ was raised from the dead through the glory of the Father, so we, too, might walk in newness of life." These verses teach Christians that water baptism does not save. Instead, water baptism is a copy of salvation. Water baptism is a symbolic portrayal of our spiritual union with Christ. Many passages in the New Testament teach that salvation precedes baptism.[9] We read in 1 Cor 1:17, "For Christ did not send me to baptize, but to preach the gospel, not in cleverness of speech, so that the cross of Christ would not be made void." This clarifies that baptism is not required for salvation, but is a step of obedience for Christians. Paul sometimes baptized people, but in 1 Cor 1:17 he makes it clear that baptism was not necessary for salvation.

Now back to 1 Peter. The ark followed Noah's faith; the ark was not Noah's faith. Baptism follows faith; but baptism is not faith. How do I know this? Peter tells us that what saves is "not the removal of dirt from the flesh." This was Peter's way of saying, "Hey guys and gals I'm not literally talking about water!" That's why we say the physical act of baptism is an act of obedience. It is good, it is important, but it is not required.

The third characteristic Peter teaches us about suffering is that *we prepare for suffering knowing God will sustain us through the suffering he allows*. In his fantastic book titled *Suffering*, pastor and author Paul David Tripp writes,

> Suffering powerfully highlights what has always been true—we were not created for independent living. Suffering exposes our weaknesses, our blindness, and our lack of control. Suffering preaches that our lives are a community project. Suffering reminds us that God's grace doesn't work to propel our independence but to deepen our vertical and horizontal dependence. The strong, independent, self-made person is a delusion. Everyone needs help and assistance. Everyone has learned at the feet of someone else. Everyone is strengthened by others. To fight community, to quest for self-sufficiency, is not only a denial of your spiritual need; it's a denial of your humanity. Suffering is a messenger telling us that to be human is to be dependent.[10]

9. Acts 2:38; 8:12; 9:18; 10:47; 16:14–15, 31–33; 18:8; 19:5.
10. Tripp, *Suffering*, 190.

Suffering teaches us to depend on God. Just as Noah and seven others were kept safe in the ark by God and just as Jesus was brought back to life from the dead by God, we, too, need to remember God will sustain us and protect us through the suffering he allows us to endure. I was in tears one Sunday morning about two months after my hospital stay. Each Sunday that passed I felt more and more tired. While I thought I would be getting stronger and return back to my normal self, I seemed to be getting weaker and weaker. Each Sunday morning I felt more tired than the last. One Sunday morning I remember standing in our kitchen and I could barely keep my eyes open, let alone stand for forty minutes and deliver a sermon. I briefly considered finding someone to preach for me on Sunday mornings. The thought of not being able to do one of my favorite things almost broke me. But, it was during that time I leaned on God more and relied on his strength more than my own. I started limiting my schedule, saying no to extra ministry requests, and experienced God's sustaining strength when I felt I had no strength of my own. It has been almost two years and I can honestly say God has carried me through every situation I've encountered. When I was discouraged, he uplifted me. When I was tired, he sent someone to lighten my workload.

But how do we rely on God's strength? When we place our faith in Christ we experience a spiritual resurrection at the moment of faith. In that moment we die and are resurrected back to eternal life forever and nothing can change that. Salvation in Christ is analogous to Noah and the ark that protected him and his family. Just as the ark was a safe haven for Noah and his family in the midst of God's judgment, our baptism with Christ is a safe haven for us in the midst of the wicked and hostile world in which we live.

If there is one thing that has surprised me in my recent experience of suffering it is how God has sustained me through the suffering he has allowed. I've preached sermons with a small trash bag on the floor next to the pulpit because I was so nauseous that I was afraid I might vomit in the middle of a sermon. I've visited church members in the hospital while I felt so terrible that I thought I should be admitted to that same hospital because I had so much pain in my gut. I've met with people in my office wondering how I would stay awake because I was so tired. God has sustained me and I trust he will continue in the future.

As Peter writes, he's describing what Christ did in his death, what Christ accomplished in his resurrection, and next Peter describes the ascension of Christ.

CHRIST'S SUMMIT

Peter tells us about Jesus, "who is at the right hand of God, having gone into heaven, after angels and authorities and powers had been subjected to Him" (1 Pet 3:22). Forty days after Jesus Christ's resurrection we learn that Jesus ascended into heaven as described in Acts 1:9–11.

The accomplishment of the ascension is what Peter wants us to understand. He's essentially saying that the point of the baptism illustration is that Christ suffered unjustly with his hope for future glory. And if he did that, we, too, may suffer wrongly but have the same hope and expectation of ultimate vindication from our suffering just like Christ did.

The fourth characteristic Peter teaches us about suffering is that *as Christians we will experience ultimate vindication from our suffering*. Christ suffered wrongfully, but still had a future hope of deliverance from that suffering. We might suffer wrongfully, but we, too, have a future hope of deliverance from that suffering. Jesus was not a victim, he was a victor. The tomb was nothing more than a motel room for a man in transit. Like Jesus, our suffering we experience is nothing but a motel room for our physical bodies as we are in transit.

As the late Warren Wiersbe has written, "We do not fight *for* victory, but *from* victory."[11] The apostle Paul told the believers in Ephesus, "But God, being rich in mercy, because of His great love with which He loved us, even when we were dead in our

11. Wiersbe, *Be Hopeful*, 107.

transgressions, made us alive together with Christ (by grace you have been saved), and raised us up with Him, and seated us with Him in the heavenly places in Christ Jesus" (Eph 2:4–6). The truth we need to hold onto is this: we might be encountering a difficult situation here on earth, but spiritually we're sitting with Christ victorious. We must never forget that even during dark, depressing days.

Sometimes in our suffering we can do nothing but wait patiently. Let me remind you to be patient in your suffering, just like Jesus experienced. I told you I wanted to return to Georgianna's story because she experienced ultimate vindication in her situation. She endured nine months of legal battles to get her three kids back. The nine months climaxed in a court appearance with a judge and no jury. The prosecuting attorney from CPS shared his arguments against Georgianna and her husband. And Georgianna was surprised that after the prosecuting attorney was done, the judge said, "I don't need to hear the defense's side." The judge then dismissed the case, smacked his gavel, and said "You can have your three kids back." The CPS case was so weak the judge didn't want to hear the defense's arguments. Georgianna later learned that after that doctor's visit with her daughter another doctor in another department saw the X-ray, noticed the small crack in the baby's head, then called CPS and reported her for abuse. The doctor did that without meeting Georgianna or seeing her daughter. Georgianna was a good and loving mom, but she had to endure a bad situation.

She experienced ultimate vindication from her suffering. Eventually, she got her kids back, her criminal history was removed, and she was able to return to work. She experienced ultimate vindication from her suffering while she was on earth.

Some of us will experience vindication while we're on earth, but some of us won't until we are in heaven with Jesus. That's why we need to prepare for suffering knowing God will sustain us through the suffering he allows. We also need to proclaim victory over those who insult, ridicule, and cause our suffering.

Sometimes unjust suffering occurs. Christ experienced it and we do too. Some of you might be experiencing unjust suffering right now. You might be thinking, "I raised my kids in church and taught them to love God, now they have walked away and it hurts so bad." Or perhaps you are perplexed as you reflect, "I worked hard, did what I was asked to do, then my job didn't promote me and I'm so discouraged." Or maybe you feel, "I've done my best to be a good Christian wife my whole life, yet my husband is still terrible. Why?"

But our hope and comfort comes from this. First, we must recognize that we as Christians experience unrighteous suffering just like Christ did. Second, we proclaim victory over those who insult, ridicule, and cause us suffering. Third, we prepare for suffering knowing God will sustain us through the suffering he allows. And fourth, we will experience ultimate vindication from our suffering either on earth or in heaven.

I hope we can find comfort in Georgianna's story where the judge threw out the case before the defense even spoke because it was illegitimate. As we read these verses it's easy to be confused and get lost. I hope we've not done that. Instead, I hope we see that Jesus Christ's ultimate victory (in spite of temporary persecution) should be an encouragement to any suffering disciple of the Savior.

4

Suffering Without Sin

When we place our faith in Jesus things change. They should change spiritually, behaviorally, and relationally.

Things change not just at conversion but as we grow and mature in our faith; our relationship with God deepens. The language we use often changes. How we handle disappointment and anger improves. The manner in which we spend money or what we spend our money on changes. The time we spend watching TV or scrolling social media is altered. The way in which we use substances such as alcohol or drugs will change too.

What does it look like to place our faith in Jesus Christ and step away from certain behaviors or specific people? Is it hard to separate ourselves from people that live a lifestyle contrary to the lifestyle God teaches in Scripture? How do we maintain a relationship with people if we no longer do the things we once did with them? How will they treat us when we no longer do the things with them that we used to do with them?

In two previous chapters we've seen that suffering happens sometimes when we do good (1 Pet 3:13–17) and suffering requires that we prepare for it, proclaim Christ in it, and expect vindication from it (1 Pet 3:18–22). In this chapter I want us to recognize that when we walk away from our old life and walk with God we will experience suffering from the people that we used to walk with. One of our temptations, when suffering comes, is to revert back to our behavior before we placed our faith in Christ. During trials we often are tempted to look for something to satisfy us and to ease the pain we are going through. Peter prepares his readers for that temptation by sharing three realities of suffering. The first concerns our attitude.

ATTITUDE

Armed for Suffering

As Peter teaches on suffering he wants his readers to be armed for the suffering ahead: "Therefore, since Christ has suffered in the flesh, arm yourselves also with the same purpose, because he who has suffered in the flesh has ceased from sin" (1 Pet 4:1). The word *therefore*[12] tells us that Peter is going to apply the principles of 1 Pet 3:19–22 to the readers' current lives. He does this by using Christ's example, "since Christ has suffered in the flesh." This describes Jesus's physical suffering (1 Pet 2:21, 23; 3:17–18), which ended in death.

Peter also applies the principles of 1 Pet 3:19–22 to the readers lives by exhorting them to "arm yourselves also with the same purpose." This is the command of the paragraph. The phrase "arm yourselves" is translated from a word only used one time in the New Testament. The Greek word *hoplisasthe*[13] is used in writings outside Scripture to refer to soldiers putting on armor. In Peter's exhortation about our attitude he says we should arm ourselves, "with the same purpose." The New Living Translation and New International Version don't use "purpose" but instead use the word "attitude," which I like a little better. The word here, *ennoian*,

12. The word *therefore* is translated from the Greek word *oun*, which is an inferential conjunction. BDAG, s.v. "oun."

13. Paul teaches the same principle but uses a different word in Rom 13:12; 2 Cor 6:7; Eph 6:10, 17; 1 Thess 5:8; Col 3:12.

comes from two words "in" (*en*) and "mind" (*nous*).[14] Peter believes his readers need to mentally prepare for the suffering ahead.

If any of the disciples knew that persecution and trouble would come to followers of Jesus Christ it was Peter. In the Gospel of John, Jesus told Peter, "Truly, truly, I say to you, when you were younger, you used to gird yourself and walk wherever you wished; but when you grow old, you will stretch out your hands and someone else will gird you, and bring you where you do not wish to go" (John 21:18). John then adds a comment explaining, "Now this He [Jesus] said, signifying by what kind of death he [Peter] would glorify God. And when He had spoken this, He said to him, 'Follow Me!'" (John 21:19). Jesus predicted Peter's suffering and death that would happen under Nero—the emperor of the Roman Empire—in AD 64.

Thus far Peter has told us about Christ's example, he has given us an exhortation, and next he reveals something for us to enjoy. Peter writes, "Because he who has suffered in the flesh has ceased from sin" (1 Pet 4:1c). Peter tells us suffering removes the power of sin. If we suffer—and we have an attitude about suffering like Christ did—then that gives us a level of victory over sin. Thus when someone suffers for doing right, he has made a clear break from sin.

Abandoned Sin

Peter wants his readers to be armed for the suffering ahead but also to abandon sin, "so as to live the rest of the time in the flesh no longer for the lusts of men, but for the will of God" (1 Pet 4:2). This verse explains the last phrase of verse 1 about what it means to be finished with sin. In this verse I need to point out that *flesh* is used differently by Peter than Paul. Paul used the word *flesh* as a metaphor to describe the sinful nature all human beings have;[15] Peter uses *flesh* to describe mortal life on earth, not sinful life on

14. BDAG, s.v. "ennoia."

15. See Rom 7:18; 8:3; 9:8; Gal 5:19–21; 6:7–9; Eph 2:3.

earth. The word *flesh* in Peter's writings describes literal tissue as a physical substance that can be touched and felt, not sinful acts or the sin nature to which Paul refers.

I also need to point out the different priorities that suffering brings into our lives. Peter reveals that suffering removes the "lusts of men." Those lusts—as we'll learn about in 1 Pet 4:3—characterize our pre-Christian past (1 Pet 1:14) and the worldly connection that we no longer belong to (1 Pet 2:11). With that established, Peter makes a contrast between "the lusts of men" and "for the will of God." Following God's will is one of the reasons Peter writes this letter. In 1 Pet 2:15 we read, "For such is the will of God that by doing right you may silence the ignorance of foolish men." In the next chapter Peter reveals, "For it is better, if God should will it so, that you suffer for doing what is right rather than for doing what is wrong" (1 Pet 3:17). And in 1 Pet 4:19 he instructs, "Therefore, those also who suffer according to the will of God shall entrust their souls to a faithful Creator in doing what is right." As you can see, knowing and following God's will is a repeated theme in this letter.

When reading 1 Pet 4:1–2 the first reality we must recognize is *suffering removes the power of sin*. One study Bible I like to use says, "Such suffering enables one to straighten out his priorities. Sinful desires and practices that once seemed important now seem insignificant when one's life is in jeopardy. Serious suffering for Christ advances the progress of sanctification."[16] That study Bible reveals that even though we are saved, God might use suffering for our sanctification.

In 1 Pet 4:1 we read that "he who has suffered in the flesh has ceased from sin." That phrase "ceased from sin" is classified by Greek scholars as an ablatival genitive that involves the notion of separation.[17] This Greek construction can be translated as "out of" or "away from" or "from."[18] An example of this type of genitive is

16. *NASB*, 1817.

17. Specifically, it's a "Genitive of Separation." See Wallace, *Greek Grammar*, 107.

18. Wallace, *Greek Grammar*, 108.

in 1 Pet 3:21 where Peter says water removes dirt *from* the body. Another example is how I moved *from* Texas in 2016 after I graduated from seminary there. I left *from* Texas and have never been back there. So here in 1 Pet 4:1–2, when Peter writes "ceased from sin" it describes how suffering has separated someone from sin. It's akin to blocking someone on your cell phone or removing them from your list of friends on Facebook. It's a way to say something is no longer part of your life and how you have no connection with it.

Suffering has a way of steeling us. The word *steel* can be used as a noun, verb, or adjective in English. As a verb it means "to cause to resemble steel (as in looks or hardness)" or "to fill with resolution or determination."[19] I believe suffering steels us to a stronger devotion to God and lessens our desire to sin. Suffering helps us get more focused on God and his priorities, it prevents us from getting distracted by sinful activities, and it keeps us walking closely with God because we must rely on him to endure our trials. In this way, suffering focuses us. Like a race horse with blinders on the sides of its eyes so it focuses only on what is ahead, suffering focuses our attention on God and his priorities while decreasing the distraction of sin. Suffering steels us in our desire to separate from sinful habits like foul language, uncontrollable anger, careless spending of money, gluttony, excessive drinking of alcohol, binge watching TV, and drug use.

I think this might be the reason we often see the church flourish in persecuted countries. In countries such as North Korea, Somalia, Yemen, Libya, and Sudan the church is severely persecuted.[20] Yet the church often flourishes, I think, because their suffering steels them, strengthens them, and solidifies their faith. Serious suffering advances the progress of sanctification and demonstrates our faith to unbelievers. As Joni Eareckson Tada has written, "Suffering's very purpose is to turn us from our sin and makes us like Christ."[21] Suffering will do that for us.

19. *Merriam-Webster*, s.v. "steel."

20. According to Open Doors those five countries have the highest amounts of persecution against Christians. See "2025 World Watch List."

21. Tada, *Her Story*, 204.

Our faith and our way of life as Christians affects others and causes them to respond in a specific way. Peter describes that next for his readers.

ANTAGONISM

In 1 Pet 4:1–2, Peter shared the attitude that we need to have in our suffering. Therefore we armed ourselves for what awaits us and abandoned the sin among us. In this way, the first reality we learned is that suffering removes the power of sin. Peter next transitions from our attitude (internal) to the antagonism (external) we face in suffering.

Our Pastime

Peter references his readers' previous life in sin before becoming a Christian when he writes, "For the time already past is sufficient for you to have carried out the desire of the Gentiles, having pursued a course of sensuality, lusts, drunkenness, carousing, drinking parties and abominable idolatries" (1 Pet 4:3). The phrase "the time already past" references the behavior and old habits before Christ came into his readers' lives.

In addition to the past, Peter also describes their practices: "the desire of the Gentiles, having pursued a course of sensuality, lusts, drunkenness, carousing, drinking parties and abominable idolatries." Lets note a few things about the desires of the Gentiles that Peter describes using "sensuality, lusts, drunkenness, carousing, drinking parties, and abominable idolatries." It might not appear this way in English, but all six Greek words are in the plural. In the plural form they describe the common and regular practices in the past that are no longer part of the believers' lives now.[22] These gatherings were not sophisticated gatherings of social interaction; these were wild and frenzied drinking bouts that included

22. *NET*, 2313.

promiscuity.[23] Think of the college fraternity or sorority house that seems to have more drinking and partying than learning and studying. That is the image Peter describes here.

Our Persecutors

In addition to describing our pastime, Peter also describes our persecutors when he writes, "In all this, they are surprised that you do not run with them into the same excesses of dissipation, and they malign you; but they will give account to Him who is ready to judge the living and the dead" (1 Pet 1:4–5).[24] Our departure from the sinful lifestyle is going to lead to suffering caused from others. Our new lifestyle is going to cause abuse from friends and family, neighbors, or coworkers.

We learn these persecutors will slander us. When Peter writes, "In all this" (v. 4), I think he refers to the change of behavior. Peter tells us these persecutors "are surprised that you do not run with them into the same excesses of dissipation, and they malign you" (v. 4). The people that we used to do things with are surprised, resentful, and offended by our departure from their lifestyle. Our desire to pursue a new lifestyle indirectly rejects them and the lifestyle they've chosen to enjoy. The "excesses of dissipation" (v. 4) describe how these people think about nothing but evil. The word *malign* there could be translated as "vilify." It's the Greek word *blasphēmountes*. This word describes someone who talks badly about a person and the God whom they worship.[25]

We also learn these persecutors will suffer themselves, "but they will give account to Him who is ready to judge the living and the dead" (1 Pet 4:5). The word *but* that separates verses 4 and 5 shows those persecutors' behavior will result in punishment. They will not escape their works and words when judgment time arrives.

23. *NET*, 2313.

24. One study Bible I consulted recently accurately describes, "Sin in the believer is a burden which afflicts him rather than a pleasure which delights him." MacArthur, *MacArthur Study Bible*, 1915.

25. Osborne, "1 Peter," 234.

That word for "give account" has a literal meaning of "pay back."[26] These persecutors are adding charges to a credit card that they will never be able to pay off. Those that pursue evil (v. 3) and malign believers (v. 4) are amassing a debt against God that they can never pay back. All of the unsaved—whether they are alive or deceased—will be brought for judgment before Jesus in what's called "the great white throne judgment" in Rev 20:11–15. Essentially, Peter's saying, "God will condemn them, so don't give in to them." It's hard to endure the suffering they are causing, but don't give in to them. Remember God will pay them back.

When reading 1 Pet 4:3–5, the second reality we must recognize is *suffering sometimes is a result from our departure from sin*. Most American cities understand the impact and culture of gangs. Once a young man or woman is in a gang it is impossible to leave the gang because of the consequences the gang members inflict on the exiting gang member. I'm afraid similar punishments (although less violent) are doled out to people that try to exit their sinful lifestyle in order to pursue a spiritual walk with Jesus. When someone decides to stop drinking alcohol, discontinue a gambling habit, or stop doing drugs, often there is a group of people that persecute and inflict suffering on the person trying to make that God-honoring decision.

I don't have Scripture to support this, but let me explain why I believe this type of persecution occurs. When the persecutors see someone no longer acting the way they do, it shows them that their behavior is wrong. The God-honoring person's good behavior sheds light on the persecutors' dark behavior. The person making a godly decision indirectly shows how others are acting wrong, thus they persecute that person and cause him suffering because of his good behavior.

When we abandon sinful habits, the people we used to sin with will change how they treat us. When we abandon foul language, uncontrollable anger, careless spending of money, gluttony, alcohol, binge watching TV, or drug use, the people that we used to do those activities with are going to persecute us. Peter tells us

26. BDAG, s.v. "apodidōmi."

that when sin goes out of our lives, suffering comes into our lives. This is the opposite of what we expect to occur.

With that said, we have something positive to look forward to in our Christian life. That's what Peter addresses next.

ANTICIPATION

Peter writes, "For the gospel has for this purpose been preached even to those who are dead, that though they are judged in the flesh as men, they may live in the spirit according to the will of God" (1 Pet 4:6). There are several interpretations of what Peter might mean when he writes about "those who are dead." I believe the correct interpretation identifies those who are dead as deceased Christians that have experienced persecution because of their faith. These are believers that have died through persecution and are considered martyrs.

In spite of suffering and eventual physical death, believers still experience life in the spirit according to the will of God. There is no death for a believer, only eternal life. While Jesus was executed in the flesh and raised by God's spirit (1 Pet 3:18), believers, too, may be punished in the flesh (physically) but will be raised by God's spirit (Rom 1:4; 8:10–11).

Thus far we have seen how suffering removes the power of sin and is a result from our departure from sin. When reading 1 Pet 4:6 the third reality we must recognize is *suffering is temporarily part of the sin of this world.* The last earthly effect of sin is physical death. In the New Testament it didn't take long for suffering to begin. Stephen became the first Christian martyr in Acts 7. Eckhard Schnabel has documented at least twenty-seven unique occurrences in the New Testament where Christians are persecuted.[27] This is important for us to consider because as Americans we struggle with suffering. We don't like it and try to avoid it. One of the early titles of this book had the word *suffering* in it. When I shared an early version of this book with an author I know he said

27. Schnabel, "Persecution of Christians."

that if he sees a book with the word *suffering* in the title he wants to run the other way.

In America we struggle with suffering because we pursue pleasure and personal freedom.[28] It's true if you think about it. In America we have dishwashers so we don't have to hand-wash dishes. We have climate-controlled buildings so that we are comfortable and don't sweat or get cold. We have garages where we park our cars to keep them protected from frost, cold weather, or extreme heat. We often have several different streaming services we pay for so that we can watch TV whenever we want. Our passion for pleasure and freedom requires us to recognize that suffering is temporarily part of the sin of this world.

In his book *Walking with God Through Pain and Suffering*, Tim Keller accurately summarizes how most Christians view suffering. Keller writes, "Often the unstated assumption of many people is that God's job is to create a world in which things benefit us."[29] If we believe God is supposed to create a world where things benefit us we will be corrected when we read Scripture. That's not what Scripture teaches us and that definitely is not what Peter teaches. In fact, Peter teaches us that suffering removes the power of sin in our lives, suffering is a result from our departure from sin that was in our lives, and suffering is temporarily part of the sin of this world. Suffering removes sin's power in our lives and steels us to God's purpose in our lives.

28. Keller, *Walking with God*, 22.

29. Keller, *Walking with God*, 115.

5

Essential Actions in Suffering

When we experience suffering it's easy to feel discouraged, have doubt, and want to give up in our spiritual walk with God. Nothing is more disheartening than suffering. Another failed pregnancy test. Another bill that's more than the money in the bank. Another bad test result from our doctor. Another "We don't have work for you" notice from our employer. Another "I don't know how to help you" from the doctor. Another "We've decided to hire another candidate" from a prospective employer.

When we read Peter's words about suffering, we realize the difficulty we have in front of us. Suffering is hard to endure. But what will get us through suffering? How does a church survive a pastor who commits extreme sin and wounds the church? How does a family make it through the death of a child? How does a marriage survive the loss of a job or financial hardship? It is in these various circumstances that Peter teaches us how to get through the suffering that we are enduring.

In previous chapters, we learned that a faithful life lived as a Christian leads to slander and suffering that gives an opportunity for a spoken witness about our hope as Christians (1 Pet 3:13–17). Next we learned that suffering occurs in our lives just like Christ experienced suffering, so we need to expect it, prepare for it, proclaim Christ in it, and trust we will experience ultimate vindication from it (1 Pet 3:18–22). In our last chapter, we learned that when we walk away from our old life and walk with God we will experience suffering from the people that we used to walk with (1 Pet 4:1–6).

Peter transitions in 1 Pet 4:6 from the topic of death (in which he described how some Christians have died and perhaps even been martyred for their faith) and then tells his readers how to live right now. Essentially, he tells them that in times of crisis the church needs each other.

In 1 Pet 4:7–11, Peter reveals that a church body needs sound minds and steadfast action along with spoken words in suffering. In these verses Peter will show us the motivation for those actions (v. 7a), the ministry we have (vv. 7b–11a), and a mark we should be shooting for (v. 11b). Let's first start with the motivation we should have.

MOTIVATION

Peter reveals our incentive for our actions. He writes, "The end of all things is near" (1 Pet 4:7a). The word for "near" is the Greek word *ēngiken*, which is regularly used in Scripture to describe the coming of Christ and his kingdom (Matt 3:2; Mark 1:15; Luke 10:9). It refers to Christ's second coming and the doctrine of imminency.[1]

The doctrine of imminency is this: Christ could return at any moment, so we are to be ready. Imminency was taught by Paul (Rom 13:11), James (Jas 5:8), John (1 John 2:18), and the author of Hebrews (Heb 13:11).

The important thing about imminency is that it has ethical implications for us living today. It effects how we live today because of the suddenness and unexpectedness that Christ could come at any moment. The late John Walvoord wrote in his book *Every Prophecy of the Bible*, "The fact that life will not go on forever should be an encouragement to Christians who are going through

1. BDAG, s.v. "engizō."

deep trouble. A Christian's pilgrimage on earth is temporary and soon may be cut short by the rapture of the church. This should serve as a stimulus to faithful service and enduring where persecutions and trials may be the lot of an individual Christian."[2] Anticipating the arrival of Christ affects our attitudes and actions. We shouldn't be lazy daydreamers.

When hearing about the *end times* or *return of Christ* sometimes we think about weirdos that stand on street corners with signs reading "The End Is Near," or preachers that sensationalize modern events to sell books about how to survive the antichrist or avoid the mark of the beast. But Peter has a different approach to the end times. He gives us practical exhortations and prudent warnings that affect our lives within a church body.

MINISTRY

Thus far Peter has told us about our motivation (the end is near); now he tells us about the ministry we must have in suffering. Peter shares that our instruction and application is to serve in God's strength.

Whole and Well Mind

He writes, "Therefore, be of sound judgment and sober spirit for the purpose of prayer" (1 Pet 4:7:b). It's important to remember the two contexts in which Peter writes this. One context is suffering (larger context) and another context is the return of Christ (smaller context). Peter advises us not to "freak out" when suffering comes and don't "lose our brain."

I heard a Christian share that the Charlie Brown Christmas movie being removed from public TV was evidence of cancel culture and a sign of the end times. (However, it was removed from public TV because Apple purchased the rights to show it exclusively on their streaming platform.) Another Christian told

2. Walvoord, *Every Prophecy*, 507.

me he believed microchips placed in dogs are a precursor to that same thing happening to humans under the reign of the antichrist and will be the mark of the beast. (However, Rev 13:16 says the mark will be "*on* their right hand or *on* their forehead," not *in* their body.)[3] During the COVID pandemic I was working at a Christian bookstore and someone told me that the change shortage was a sign the government was trying to move us to a cashless society and was a sign of the end times. (There was a change shortage because many retail stores were forced to close, which meant change was sitting in safes and store registers and was not being circulated.)

While enduring suffering we must *stay grounded and use sound judgment*. We should not be swept away by emotions or passions. We don't want to be date setters or sign lookers that pay more attention to news headlines than God's word. We might not always understand what we see occurring in our world, but we stay humble and stay grounded in those moments.

We must be clear headed and focused. I'm guessing you know the dangers of driving on a curvy mountain road. Carefully driving a dangerous road like that requires you stay focused on the road in front of you as well as anticipating what you see approaching. If you stare at the edge of the cliff, your hands naturally steer that direction. But if you focus on the road ahead, you stay safely on course. Where you set your eyes determines where you go. When we are in the midst of suffering it's common to have trouble staying focused on the task at hand. For us as Christians this means living right and sharing the gospel with those that need to hear it before Christ returns. It means we grip Christ stronger during tough times because we need someone to hold onto. We should be ready for Christ to come but also make plans if he doesn't come back immediately.

3. Emphasis added.

Warm Heart

Next Peter writes, "Above all, keep fervent in your love for one another, because love covers a multitude of sins" (1 Pet 4:8). The phrase "above all" is a gentle reminder that in light of the 613 laws of the Old Testament and everything Jesus taught, do this! Love is important, especially as we approach the end times, because Jesus said that people's love will grow cold (Matt 24:12) and Paul wrote people will be lovers of self in the end times (2 Tim 3:1).

It appears that Peter loosely paraphrases Prov 10:12: "Hatred stirs up strife, but love covers all transgressions." Peter's describing a compassionate and covering love of others. He's telling us to extend forbearance toward others.

The phrase "keep fervent" is translated from the Greek word *ektenē*. It's only used two times in the New Testament. The idea conveyed in this word is "being persevering, with implication that one does not waver in one's display of interest or devotion."[4] It's often translated as "eager, earnest."[5] The picture that comes to mind when using this word is like a horse at full gallop or a runner stretching for the finish line.

When enduring suffering we must *continue to love each other*. Love is easy when life is easy. But love is hard when life gets hard. Specifically, love is difficult when we endure hardship. Suffering puts a squeeze on everything. We're less patient, less understanding, less graceful, and less loving when enduring trials.

In 2014 I was inside our apartment in Grand Prairie, Texas, when someone began pounding on our front door. When I opened the door the maintenance man for the apartment complex told me the apartment had caught fire and that I needed to leave the building immediately. I grabbed two armfuls of important documents and family heirlooms, but everything else my wife and I owned was lost in the fire. The following days and weeks were a stressful time as we had to find a new place to live, purchase new clothes, and rebuild our lives in addition to attending school and working.

4. BDAG, s.v. "ektenēs."
5. BDAG, s.v. "ektenēs."

A few weeks after the apartment fire I was still trying to get clothes that fit, so I decided to go to the clothes closet that was often advertised as a free resource for students at the seminary I attended. The store was only open on Wednesday for a couple hours. Since my classes were on Tuesdays and Thursdays, I made an extra trip to the school campus on a Wednesday. I drove thirty minutes to campus, battling Dallas traffic in the rain, and when I arrived I learned the clothes closet was closed that day. I went to the student services desk in another building and inquired about why it was closed on the day and at the time it was advertised to be open. The young woman explained that the store staff had decided not to be open that day. After driving to campus on a day I normally would not have driven there, and battling traffic and the rain, I replied, "Well I wish I would have know that before I drove from Grand Prairie through the rain to come here!" The woman kindly apologized again and I left to drive home.

I have often regretted my behavior in that moment. To act that way and say what I said was uncharacteristic for me. I normally am easy going, lighthearted, patient, and gracious to others. During that difficult time I did not act like myself. I had endured a few very stressful weeks and it showed in how I treated that woman.

I share that story because it shows the stress suffering puts on us. When we endure suffering we often are impatient and unwilling to extend grace to others.

During times of suffering we must slow down and consciously remind ourselves to be loving. When enduring pain and suffering we are not ourselves. When we are stressed and pressured we don't act how we normally act. Because of that we need to intentionally show love to others. We might need to ask our spouse or a friend to remind us to be loving.

Continuing to love others, in the midst of suffering, requires a biblical application of love. Biblical love is a covering of sin. It's not ignoring sin, but loving in spite of sin.[6]

6. There are sins, of course, that require discipline if the church member is unrepentant (Matt 18:15–18; 1 Cor 5). But Peter tells us to cover all other sins.

Thus far Peter has told us we need a whole and well mind that keeps us grounded in order to use sound judgment. He's also told us we need a warm heart to continue loving each other in the midst of our struggles. Next Peter tells us about the hospitality we should offer to others within our home.

Welcoming Home

In 1 Pet 4:9 we read, "Be hospitable to one another without complaint." When we read about hospitality it's important we understand the context of the first century in which these words were written. Hospitality was vital in the first century because hotels and inns were rare. The hotels and inns that were available had a poor reputation and were considered unsafe. Some New Testament commentators say hotels and inns were brothels as well as hotels.[7]

In the Mediterranean world it was an honor to be a host. Refusing someone's offer of hospitality was considered an insult to the host's generosity. Usually a host would offer food, a place to sleep, and help the travelers on their way with money or items necessary for travel. A traveler might stay with a host for three days or as long as a week (as seen by Paul in Acts 9:9; 20:6; 21:4, 7; 28:14). Hosting travelers was also a generational obligation as family members expected hospitality from a previous generation's kindness in the past.[8]

With a correct understanding of hospitality in the first century it's also important we understand the context of first-century Christians. It was important for them to stay away from any association with sexual promiscuity. Hospitality among Christians was a key activity that enabled mission work to occur (3 John 5). Hospitality was even more important because sometimes the persecution and suffering that Christians experienced caused families to have to find somewhere else to live.

7. Keener, *1 Peter*, 317–21.

8. Keener, *1 Peter*, 317–21.

That context is important for us to understand because we often view hospitality as something that costs money, takes time, and is inconvenient. Hospitality should be extended to friends but also to strangers too! When Peter writes "be hospitable," the text could literally be translated as "be friendly to strangers" or have "love for strangers."[9]

While enduring suffering *we must keep hosting others*. When suffering comes it's easy to become inward focused. Three of my seven days in the hospital were spent in a shared room with another man about my age. What a dream for a preacher to have a captive audience that can't leave! But, I was so nauseous and in so much pain I never asked the man about his faith and I never shared the gospel with him. The point is this: when in suffering it is easy to focus on ourselves and not think about others.

When we are in pain we often don't want to be kind, welcoming, and hospitable to others. When tight on money we don't want to purchase food for others that need it. When tight on time we don't want to stop and help someone fix a flat tire. But Peter's telling us, even when in difficult times, we need to help others through hospitality.

We might feel inadequate for hospitality because of the small size of our home, the cleanliness of it, or how others decorate and entertain well. Sometimes Christians are not hospitable because we confuse hospitality with entertainment. In an article in *Moody* magazine Karen Maines accurately points out that entertainment and hospitality are different:

- Entertaining says, "I want to impress you with my home, my clever decorating, my gourmet cooking." Hospitality, seeking to minister, says, "this home is a gift from my master. I use it as He desires. . . ." Hospitality aims to serve.
- Entertainment subtly declares, "This home is mine, an expression of my personality. Look, please, and admire." Hospitality whispers, "What is mine is yours."

9. Keener, *1 Peter*, 317.

- Entertaining looks for a payment—the words, "My, isn't she a remarkable hostess. . . ." With no thought of reward, hospitality takes pleasure in giving, doing, loving, serving.
- The model for entertaining is the slick women's magazines with their alluring pictures of foods and rooms. The model for hospitality is the word of God. Christ sanctifies our simple fare and makes it holy, useful.[10]

Our goal as Christians is to offer hospitality, not entertainment. We don't need to feel an obligation to entertain, but to be hospitable. We can be hospitable even if our kitchen table serves as the home school instruction area, the craft area, or game table. The first small group Bible study that my wife and I hosted was in our small one-bedroom apartment. It certainly was not an ideal place to entertain ten people, but it was well suited for hospitality.

We never know what good might come out of our faithfulness to be hospitable. One of the most powerful preachers of the twentieth century was W. A. Criswell. He was converted to Christ because of his parents' hospitality. When Criswell was ten years old, a preacher came to a revival that his church was hosting. Criswell's mother offered to host the preacher in their home during his two-week stay. The visiting preacher was Rev. John Hicks. Criswell would sit next to Hicks at dinner, walk to and from church with Hicks, and regularly asked Hicks questions. By the time Hicks left town Criswell asked Jesus Christ to be his Savior.[11] Hospitality is something we are all called to do and we never know how God might use our home or us to serve his kingdom through our hospitality.

Thus far Peter has told us that when in the midst of suffering we need a whole and well mind that helps us stay grounded and use sound judgment. He's told us we need a warm heart that continues loving each other. And he's encouraged us to maintain a welcoming home in which we keep hosting others. Last, he says

10. Karen Maines, quoted in Morgan, *Preacher's Sourcebook*, 452.

11. Morgan, *Preacher's Sourcebook*, 453.

we need working hands that stay busy in the midst of suffering and pain.

Working Hands

There are four passages in the New Testament that teach us about the spiritual gifts given to believers (Rom 12:6–8; 1 Cor 12:4–11; Eph 4:11; 1 Pet 4:10–11). Peter's purpose in writing about spiritual gifts is not to describe the gifts but to deploy us in using our gifts. He writes, "As each one has received a special gift, employ it in serving one another as good stewards of the manifold grace of God. Whoever speaks is to do so as one who is speaking the utterances of God; whoever serves is to do so as one who is serving by the strength which God supplies" (1 Pet 4:10–11a). Let's note a few things Peter teaches us about spiritual gifts.

Peter teaches us that spiritual gifts are individually given. In the first part of verse 10 he writes, "As each one has received a special gift." The phrase "special gift" is the Greek noun *charisma*.[12] That noun comes from the verb *charizomai*, meaning "to give graciously,"[13] which is also related to the noun *charis* which means "grace."[14] Spiritual gifts are a generous and gracious act of God.

Peter teaches us that spiritual gifts are community focused. In the middle of verse 10 he writes, "Employ it in serving one another." When we receive a spiritual gift from God the spiritual gift is not about us. The gift is not given to boost our egos or to enhance our self-esteem. Spiritual gifts are God's investments into his members, and he expects a return on his investment by us using those gifts to serve others.

Peter teaches us that spiritual gifts are heavenly enabled. In the last part of verse 10 he writes, "As good stewards of the manifold grace of God." This reminds us again that spiritual gifts are something we receive that we did not earn. God's grace not only

12. BDAG, s.v. "charisma."

13. BDAG, s.v. "charizomai."

14. BDAG, s.v. "charis."

rescues us from sin but also equips us to serve. This requires us to be stewards of what we are given. That word *steward* is a term we don't use often today. A steward in the New Testament was one who served as a house manager. He had no wealth of his own but he distributed the wealth of his master according to the will and direction of the master.[15] We might compare the job of a first-century steward to that of a payroll administrator within a modern organization. A payroll administrator does not possess the wealth of the company for himself, but he is responsible to distribute that wealth on behalf of the company that decides who gets what amounts. In a similar way, we are stewards of God's spiritual gifts.

Peter teaches us that spiritual gifts are actively deployed. In the first half of verse 11 Peter writes, "Whoever speaks is to do so as one who is speaking the utterances of God; whoever serves is to do so as one who is serving by the strength which God supplies." Again, Peter's purpose in writing about spiritual gifts is not to describe all the gifts but to convince us to deploy our gifts. Peter encourages us to use our gifts by describing them in two broad categories. When he writes "speaks" I believe he's referring to the teaching and exhorting gifts. When he writes "serves" I believe he's referring to the leading, serving, and mercy gifts.[16] This distinction is based on Acts 6:2–4 when the apostles wanted to focus on preaching (speaking) so they appointed deacons to care for widows (serving).

While enduring suffering *we must use our spiritual gifts.* Sometimes spiritual gifts can be confusing among the different passages. Some people say we have a primary spiritual gift and another secondary spiritual gift. Some people say the gifts are offices and activities. I've even heard people teach that the spiritual gifts are like colors of a wheel and we each mix them together differently.

15. Raymer, "1 Peter," 853–54.

16. The "speaks" would correspond to what Paul says in Romans are "teaching" (Rom 12:7b) and "exhorting" (Rom 12:8a). The "serves" would correspond to what Paul says in Romans are "leading" (Rom 12:8b), "service" (Rom 12:7a), and "mercy" (Rom 12:8c).

While those are all legitimate ways to interpret the gifts, I must admit I think I misinterpreted 1 Pet 4:10–11a for many years. If we pay attention to the context of these two verses—with what occurs before and after—we notice that spiritual gifts are described within the context of what to do when encountering suffering. When we are going through suffering we get through it by using our spiritual gifts!

This explanation from Grant Osborne is relevant for our discussion of spiritual gifts used while in suffering:

> The purpose of gifts is never to exalt the person but rather to serve the community. So every Christian . . . is given exactly the gifts God wants, and each is meant to use them for the benefit of the church and the glory of God. This leads to the interdependence of all believers. We need each other, to be the dispensers and also the recipients of the gifts God has given to the church through his people. The church is a family with each member supporting the others by using their gifts—not for status but for the enrichment of others. Gifts do not confer status; they confer responsibility.[17]

Osborne's description of the role of spiritual gifts reminds me of a scene from *Back to the Future* when Marty McFly travels back in time from 1985 to 1955. Everything he sees around him looks different and the people act different. As Marty is walking he sees a car pull into a gas station and he hears the "ding" as the car runs over a bell strip. When the sound is heard four guys leap out from the gas station. One man checks the oil, another pumps gas, the other checks the air in the tires, and another cleans the windshield.[18] Marty's puzzled look is similar to unbelievers when they see Christians still serving and working hard while in the midst of suffering. God wants his church to be a full-service gas station with each member fulfilling a unique role and serving a unique purpose, even in the midst of severe suffering.

17. Osborne, "1 Peter," 243.

18. Zemeckis, *Back to the Future*.

At this point Peter has shared that our incentive for action in suffering is because the end is near, and our instruction and application is to serve in God's strength; last, Peter tells us that the outcome we desire is for God to be praised.

MARK

Peter continues, in verse 11, "so that in all things God may be glorified through Jesus Christ, to whom belongs the glory and dominion forever and ever. Amen" (1 Pet 4:11b). The goal is clear: God gets the credit. That word *glory* refers to the praise God deserves and *dominion* describes the power God has.

What we accomplish gives God honor and credit. Specifically, when we serve one another and speak to one another in the midst of our sufferings, God gets the credit for those things. When Elisabeth Elliot's husband was murdered by the native people he tried to reach with the gospel, God gets the credit when Elisabeth forgave them and brought them the gospel years later. When Fanny Crosby wrote more than nine thousand hymns in the nineteenth century in spite of her blindness, God gets the credit for empowering her to the magnificent work. When those things happen during our suffering, God gets the credit!

Each of these areas we've discussed are areas in which it's easy to get tentative when tough times come. We can easily make reasons not to do those things, but we have God's reasons they should be done.

It's easy to step back or step away, but Peter tells us to step forward into sound judgment and clear thinking, to step into acts of love for others, to keep hosting others in our home as ministry to strangers and friends, and to use our spiritual gifts whether as speaking or serving.

When we do those things we are obedient to God's word in suffering. When we do them we will realize that we all play a part in suffering successfully. The best part is that God will get the credit.

6

Rejoicing in Righteous Suffering

THE FIRST SUNDAY OF NOVEMBER is normally recognized as the International Day of Prayer for the Persecuted Church. In 2024 there were 4,476 Christians who "were killed for faith related reasons."[1] That's twelve persons a day, or one person every two hours. Open Doors estimates that 310 million Christians around the world are suffering "high levels of persecution" for their faith in Jesus Christ.[2] If we narrow those numbers down into geographical regions it looks like this: two out of every five believers are persecuted in Asia and one out of every five believers are persecuted in Africa.[3]

The Missionary Church says this is because "darkness hates the light, and when the light of Jesus enters, the darkness not only resists but fights to retain its territory."[4]

Those numbers should not surprise us. Jesus told his disciples, "You did not choose Me but I chose you, and appointed you that you would go and bear fruit, and that your fruit would remain. . . . If the world hates you, you know that it has hated Me before it hated you. If you were of the world, the world would love its own;

1. Open Doors, "2025 World Watch List."
2. Open Doors, "2025 World Watch List."
3. Open Doors, "2025 World Watch List."
4. Missionary Church, "Prayer for Persecuted Church."

but because you are not of the world, but I chose you out of the world, because of this the world hates you" (John 15:16a, 18–19). Jesus was describing suffering and persecution then as well as now. Paul gave a picture of this in the time of the church age: "Now I rejoice in my sufferings for your sake, and in my flesh I do my share on behalf of His body, which is the church, in filling up what is lacking in Christ's afflictions" (Col 1:24).

But if we are honest, suffering as Christians and because we are Christians is a foreign concept to most of us. How many of us were given an invitation to trust in Jesus Christ as our Savior and were told about suffering? How many of us have seen TV preachers describe how God wants to bless us and provide for us? How many of us have been told either directly or indirectly in sermons or books that God wants us to be healthy, wealthy, and prosperous?

In this chapter we will conclude the section of Peter's letter that directly addresses suffering of Christians.[5] Specifically, we will learn from 1 Pet 4:12–19 that suffering should not be caused by our sin but is something we trust God in, rejoice in, and glorify his name in. In this concluding paragraph on suffering we'll see the situation of suffering (vv. 12–14), the cause of suffering (vv. 15–16), and the response to suffering (vv. 17–19). Ultimately we will realize suffering fits into God's purposes for our lives and we will learn four steps we follow in righteous suffering.

THE SITUATION

Peter affirmed the difficult situation first-century Christians were in when he wrote, "Beloved, do not be surprised at the fiery ordeal among you, which comes upon you for your testing, as though some strange thing were happening to you; but to the degree that you share the sufferings of Christ, keep on rejoicing, so that also at the revelation of His glory you may rejoice with exultation. If

5. My broad outline for the book of 1 Peter is this: life in the Son (1:3—2:10), life in society (2:11—3:12), life in suffering (3:13—4:19), and a life in service (5:1–11).

you are reviled for the name of Christ, you are blessed, because the Spirit of glory and of God rests on you" (1 Pet 4:12–14).

Peter starts these verses with the word *Beloved*, which is a term of endearment that addresses faithful saints, not phony Christians or disobedient believers. This affectionate address prepares them for an exhortation.

The Picture

We again are reminded of the difficult situation these believers are experiencing when Peter speaks of "the fiery ordeal among you, which comes upon you for your testing" (1 Pet 4:12b). At this point we need to remember who the emperor of Rome was in AD 63 when Peter wrote this letter.

Nero was the emperor of Rome from AD 54 to 68. His mother poisoned Claudius (her husband) because she wanted Nero (her son) to rule. Nero was a stable and reasonable man early in his rule, but he became more erratic as his reign continued. Nero is famous for beginning the first extended persecution of Christians when he blamed them for a fire in the city of Rome that began on July 8 in AD 64. The aftermath of this and the persecution of Christians led to the deaths of Peter and Paul.[6]

Tacitus was a Roman historian and politician who lived AD 56–120. He's regarded by modern secular scholars as one of the greatest Roman historians. Tacitus says this about Rome in the first century:

> Nero fastened the guilt and inflicted the most exquisite tortures on a class hated for their abominations, called Christians by the populace. Christus, from whom the name had its origin, suffered the extreme penalty during the reign of Tiberius at the hands of one of our procurators, Pontius Pilatus, and a most mischievous

6. Some people say Nero started the fire because he wanted to rebuild Rome, but when the people turned against him, Nero decided to blame the Christians. Some people say Nero started the fire and always intended to blame Christians for it.

> superstition, thus checked for the moment, again broke out not only in Judaea [sic], the first source of the evil, but even in Rome. . . . Accordingly, an arrest was first made of all who pleaded guilty; then, upon their information, an immense multitude was convicted, not so much of the crime of firing the city, as of hatred against mankind. Mockery of every sort was added to their deaths. Covered with the skins of beasts, they were torn by dogs and perished, or were nailed to crosses, or were doomed to the flames and burnt, to serve as a nightly illumination, when daylight had expired. Nero offered his gardens for the spectacle, and was exhibiting a show in the circus, while he mingled with the people in the dress of a charioteer or stood aloft on a car. Hence, even for criminals who deserved extreme and exemplary punishment, there arose a feeling of compassion; for it was not, as it seemed, for the public good, but to glut one man's cruelty, that they were being destroyed.[7]

Nero's persecution of Christians is unfathomable. Nero would have garden parties at his palace and used the flames from burning Christians as light for his parties. Peter likely died in this wave of persecution that broke out in Rome under Nero that Tacitus recounts. Peter either senses this persecution is coming or has already seen it, so Peter writes this letter to believers in Asia Minor to prepare them for this type of persecution coming to them. While that's the picture of suffering, next Peter reveals our posture in suffering.

Our Posture

Peter shares, "Do not be surprised . . . as though some strange thing were happening to you" (v. 12a). Again, Peter is probably writing just before (or after) this persecution in Rome has occurred. He knows suffering for Christians is coming. The word for "surprised" here is *xenizesthe* and is the same Greek word used in 1 Pet 4:4 to describe how non-Christians are "surprised" when Christians no

7. Tacitus, *Annales* 15.44.

longer do sinful things.[8] As non-Christians are surprised that we don't sin with them, Christians should not be surprised when trials occur.

Again, Peter probably writes these words from Rome (1 Pet 5:13), probably in AD 63, shortly before the fire of Rome that instigated an intense period of persecution for the church. While there appears to be persecution occurring among the believers[9] in the Asia Minor region, this likely was a localized, unofficial persecution that caused believers trials, troubles, and suffering.

It's here in 1 Pet 4:12 that we see the first step we follow in suffering: *prepare for suffering with our minds.* People living in the United States have enjoyed a long hiatus from suffering because of faith in Jesus Christ. In America we are perhaps the least persecuted Christians in the world. That's nice, but poses a problem for us. When we face persecution or suffering we are quickly taken aback and rattled by it. But when we prepare for suffering it's easier to endure.

Seminary professor Thomas Constable writes in his commentary on 1 Peter, "Some Christians are 'surprised' when other people misunderstand, dislike, insult, and treat them harshly as they seek to carry out God's will. Peter reminded his readers that this reaction against them is not a 'strange' thing but normal Christian experience. Their persecutions were 'fiery' ordeals in the sense that they were part of God's refining process and were uncomfortable (cf. 2:11). It was for their 'testing.'"[10] That type of uncomfortable experience is what—according to Peter—should be the normal experience for us as Christians.

At this point we've learned about the picture of suffering and our posture in it; next Peter shares our practices in suffering.

8. BDAG, s.v. "xenizō."

9. M. R. Vincent makes the case based on the present tense participle *hymin ginomenē* ("comes upon you") and *hymin sumbainontos* ("happening to you") that these types of trials were already in progress. Vincent, *Word Studies*, 663.

10. Constable, *1 Peter*, 98.

Our Practices

Peter writes, "But to the degree that you share the sufferings of Christ, keep on rejoicing, so that also at the revelation of His glory you may rejoice with exultation" (1 Pet 4:13).

In this verse Peter tells us the cause of suffering: "But to the degree that you share the sufferings of Christ." I think that phrase is a subtle hint about the type of suffering his audience is enduring: unjust suffering. They might have been surprised because they hadn't done anything wrong, just as Christ had not done anything wrong, yet still suffered.

In this verse Peter gives us a command in suffering: "Keep on rejoicing." Another way to translate that phrase from Greek to English could be, "be constantly rejoicing." We rejoice in our suffering because it is through our sufferings that we identify with Christ. The apostle Paul revealed, in Phil 3:10, "that I may know Him and the power of His resurrection and the fellowship of His sufferings, being conformed to His death." Do we want to feel more connected with Jesus? Then we should endure suffering! While most people say they want to feel more connected to God, most are not willing to suffer in order to achieve that desire.

Like my author friend who says if he sees *suffering* in a book title he wants to run the other way, most Christians want to avoid suffering. For three years I worked at a Christian bookstore while serving as a part-time pastor. The books on our shelves about suffering did not sell well. We once received a large stack of "Beyond Suffering" Bibles in the New Living Translation. In three years I don't remember ever selling one of those Bibles.

It's here in 1 Pet 4:12 that we see the second step we follow in suffering: *rejoice in suffering with our words*. On this topic of rejoicing in suffering I appreciate the perspective of pastors David Walls and Max Anders:

> Joy in suffering is not a trick of the mind. Rejoicing in pain has nothing to do with deriving pleasure from being mistreated in some way. Suffering has meaning as it puts us into deeper fellowship with Jesus Christ. As this

> occurs, our level of trust in his wisdom and care in our lives increases so that we are able to rejoice. Joy, in its most sublime meaning, is a deep confidence that God is in control of every area of our lives, even the painful places. The fullness of joy comes from a deep sense of the presence of God in a person's life. Joy occurs when our pain drives us to depend on God.[11]

With these insights here's how we respond. Instead of counting the number of things we do in ministry, we need to count our persecutions because of ministry. When we share the gospel we should not count conversions, but rejections. We should not measure our success as Christians with likes on Facebook but instead with negative reactions to the Christian things we do. We should not be praised for the nice deeds we do, but should receive praise for how many complaints people make about our work done in love.

A correct view of suffering based on Scripture sees suffering as a privilege, not a penalty. Do you remember that passage from Acts 5:17–26 where Peter and other Christians were in Jerusalem performing miracles and teaching the word of God, but the high priest and Sadducees placed Peter and other Christians in jail? The high priest told Peter and his associates while they were in jail not to teach the gospel (Acts 5:27–28). Peter and the other apostles replied that they would obey God who told them to preach the gospel and they would not follow the instructions of men (Acts 5:29–32). The high priest decided to flog Peter and the apostles, then release them from custody (Acts 5:40). When Peter and the apostles were released the author of Acts says they left the high priest "rejoicing that they had been considered worthy to suffer shame for *His name*" (Acts 5:41b). Suffering, according to Scripture, is a privilege not a penalty. When someone does something that hurts us, we need to consider ourselves honored.

With our picture, posture, and practices already fleshed out, next Peter tells us about our place within suffering.

11. Walls and Anders, *I Peter*, 94.

Our Place

Peter shares, "If you are reviled for the name of Christ, you are blessed, because the Spirit of glory and of God rests on you" (1 Pet 4:14). In this verse Peter describes where we are. The word *reviled* is a term we don't use much anymore. It means "to subject to verbal abuse" or "to use abusive language." A synonym of reviled is "scold."[12] Notice some of the terms in this paragraph: "fiery ordeal" (v. 12), "testing" (v. 12), "suffering" (v. 13), and "suffer" (vv. 15, 16, 19).

In this verse Peter also describes what we receive. The word *because* describes the cause (which is suffering) and effect (spirit of glory rests on you). This likely is a reference to the Holy Spirit that we have already. Suffering is a stamp of approval by God that we are children of God. As the late Bible teacher J. Vernon McGee taught, "The greatest proof that you are a child of God is that you can endure suffering."[13]

Now that the current situation is articulated, Peter addresses the background and cause for the present situation.

THE CAUSE

Next we read the fine print. In 1 Pet 4:15–16 we learn about the cause of our suffering. "Make sure that none of you suffers as a murderer, or thief, or evildoer, or a troublesome meddler; but if anyone suffers as a Christian, he is not to be ashamed, but is to glorify God in this name" (1 Pet 4:15–16).

In verse 15 we learn about potential sins that lead to suffering. Here Peter lists the specific sins of someone who is a "murderer" or "thief." These, of course, are extreme and obvious legal infractions. Peter also lists the general sins of someone who is an "evildoer" or a "troublesome meddler." These describe moral and social offenses. That last one, "troublesome meddler," possibly describes a "busybody, one who meddles in the affairs of others."[14] I think

12. *Merriam-Webster*, s.v. "revile."

13. McGee, *1 Peter*, 92.

14. *NET*, 2314.

Peter's trying to keep us focused. He's telling us to stick with items related to the gospel and the Bible. Don't meddle in things that are not related to Scripture.

In verse 16 we learn about a positive response to suffering. Notice the two words that are contrasted here: "Christian" and "ashamed." The word *Christian* describes us who follow Jesus today, but it's a term that's only used three times in the Bible. In Scripture, Christians described themselves as "believers," "brothers," "disciples," "saints," or followers of "the way." The first two uses of the word *Christian* in the New Testament were derogatory labels other people used for disciples of Jesus (Acts 11:26; 26:28). Peter is the only Christian in the Bible that uses the term Christian, and he uses it in the same sentence about not being ashamed for being one.

It's here in 1 Pet 4:15–16 that we see the third step we follow in suffering: *glorify God in suffering with our actions*. Peter's words tell us to not feel "ashamed" but to "glorify God." We avoid shame when we know we are doing good, have a solid relationship with his people, and when we know we didn't cause or bring the suffering upon ourselves.

My mom and dad used to tell my sister and I, "Two wrongs don't make a right." It was their way of teaching us that even though your sibling did something wrong to you, it does not give you permission to do something wrong in retaliation. Peter's saying almost the same thing related to our suffering. Two wrongs don't make a right. Don't let their sin lead to your sin, which will cause your suffering. In other words, don't suffer because of sin. Don't act like an unbeliever.

For many years I was in a Toastmasters club in order to improve my public speaking. When someone first joins Toastmasters, the club matches the new person with an experienced Toastmaster for encouragement, advice, and guidance, called a mentor. Anthony was my Toastmasters mentor. When I was about to nervously stand up and walk to the podium to give my presentation Anthony would always give me the same advice: "Hey, don't mess it up!" For us as Christians, we are going to suffer for doing good. Thus we must do everything we can to avoid sin, decisions, or actions that might cause our suffering. We need to be the best Christians we can be so that we don't bring suffering into our lives for the wrong reasons. In other words, if we do suffer it should be because we are Christians, not criminals.

Peter has told us that if we rejoice in righteous suffering we must understand the situation and cause, but we also must know how to respond. That's where Peter takes us next.

THE RESPONSE

While we've seen the situation and cause of our suffering, now we get our response. As children of God, he wants us to be correctly informed about our righteous suffering.

Peter wants us to realize God's children will suffer first. "For it is time for judgment to begin with the household of God; and if it begins with us first" (1 Pet 4:17a). God was sending these trials to purge the believers and purify their faith. When Peter writes about judgment, that's not condemnation but instead it is "the purging, chastening, and purifying of the church by the loving hand of God."[15]

Peter asks rhetorical questions to help us realize God's children will suffer less: "What will be the outcome for those who do not obey the gospel of God? 'And if it is with difficulty that the righteous is saved, what will become of the godless man and the sinner?'" (1 Pet 4:17b–18). This is a point of comparison. In other words, we could say it is much more important that we endure the suffering of God as a believer while on earth than to endure the lake of fire and eternal torment in hell forever as an unbeliever. This is an argument from the lesser to the greater. If God's children are judged this amount, then how much more will those who do not love God be judged?

The last part of verse 18 is an Old Testament quotation of Prov 11:31: "If it is with difficulty that the righteous is saved." That

15. MacArthur, *MacArthur Study Bible*, 1917.

word *difficulty* describes the pain and struggles that come in the Christian life as believers follow God. It's not just a difficult situation, transaction, or moment in time, but instead describes the trials that come because someone is a Christian.

At this point we need to remember that Paul, James, and Peter use the word *salvation* slightly differently. Paul's salvation was initiation. He looks at *saved* as how you get in. James's salvation was practical or progressive. He looks at *saved* as what you do once you're in. And Peter's salvation was glorification. He looks at *saved* as a future experience to look forward to eternally.

I don't think that Peter's words in 1 Pet 4:17–18 describe how it's questionable that we are saved, but instead that if God disciplines those who love him, then he definitely is going to punish those who don't love him. This means that 1 Pet 4:18 emphasizes the point of 1 Pet 4:17, which is this: if the justified sinner is saved yet still endures great difficulty, pain, suffering, and loss, then the ungodly will experience something far greater.

Peter wants us to realize God's children will suffer first, suffer less, and God's children will find rest. "Therefore, those also who suffer according to the will of God shall entrust their souls to a faithful Creator in doing what is right" (1 Pet 4:19). This is perhaps the most important verse of the paragraph. In this verse we get an explanation. The word *therefore* is the explanation of what we do when we understand 1 Pet 4:17–18. It draws these encouragements to a conclusion and gives a command based on them. In this verse we also get identification. Peter defines his readers here as "those also who suffer according to the will of God." Peter wants his readers to make sure they don't assume they are outside the will of God just because they are suffering. We see God's will mentioned in relation to suffering in 1 Pet 3:17: "For it is better, if God should will it so, that you suffer for doing what is right rather than for doing what is wrong." We also see God's will mentioned in relation to suffering in 1 Pet 4:2: "So as to live the rest of the time in the flesh no longer for the lusts of men, but for the will of God." Those verses, along with 1 Pet 4:19, tell us as children of God that we might suffer even if we are inside of God's will for us. In this verse we also get the implication. Because of these truths, this is what we are supposed to do: "entrust their souls to a faithful Creator in doing what is right." The word *entrust* here is a term that means "entrust someone to the care or protection of someone."[16] This is the same term Jesus uses as he released his spirit into God's hands in Luke 23:46. We might think about this idea of entrusting our soul to the way sometimes we place things within a safety deposit box at a bank. Just as we would take a precious item and entrust it to a bank to protect it from harm and make sure it is not stolen, we, too, entrust our souls to God to protect us from harm. But who do we entrust it to? Our Creator who knows best the needs of his creation.

It's here in 1 Pet 4:17–19 that we see the fourth step we follow in suffering: *trust God in suffering with our soul*. Pastor and author Tim Keller was correct when he wrote, "When pain and suffering come upon us, we finally see not only that we are not in control of our lives but that we never were."[17] If we think that trusting in God means we don't have to endure suffering, then we are wrong.

Recently, I scheduled a week off from work but had no plans to travel anywhere or do anything. My wife was still planning to go to work each day and my son was going to school each day. It was supposed to be a week of rest, a chance to catch up on a few projects, and would provide some free time for me to do what I wanted to do. For more than a month I gladly anticipated this week. However, on the first day of my "rest week" some of my digestive issues started up again. I had pain in my gut, unexplained nausea, irregular bathroom trips, and honestly I just felt crummy. It was inconvenient to feel poorly, but most of all I was discouraged. How much longer will these issues continue? I thought I was getting better? I've been told rest and relaxation should help my issues but here I am supposed to rest and relax but I'm still having the same problems!

The ultimate thing that gets us through suffering is relying on God. We do this by talking to him, reading his word, and being

16. BDAG, s.v. "paratithēmi."

17. Keller, *Walking with God*, 5.

with his people. We trust God in suffering with our souls. That's what we do as Christians and that's what we sign up for when we place our faith in God.

A book I often give to people enduring tough times is Warren Wiersbe's book *The Bumps Are What You Climb On*. In that book he writes, "You cannot trust someone who is a stranger to you. You must know Jesus Christ as your own Savior and Lord if you want Him to direct you. When you surrender to Christ, then God becomes your Father, and Christ becomes your Shepherd, and the Holy Spirit becomes your Teacher; and together they direct you into the will of God."[18] What an amazing reminder that we trust God with our suffering and with our soul.

Now that we've looked at 1 Pet 4:12–19 together I want to ask you if you have entrusted your soul to God for care? Have you placed your faith in God for your salvation? Have you repented of your past sins and placed your faith in him?

Peter has taught us that becoming a follower of God isn't going to make your life better on earth, but it will make it worse. Peter has also taught us that becoming a follower of God isn't going to prevent suffering from coming into your life, but it will cause suffering in your life.

That might not sound like good news, but the good news is this: Your suffering here on earth as a believer will be less than it would be if you suffer in the future in hell forever. That's the offer provided to us, and Peter is telling us what we are signing up for when we place our faith in Jesus.

18. Wiersbe, *Bumps Are What You Climb*, 81.

7

Still Standing

Suffering is a difficult topic to discuss for Americans. We do not suffer well because we do not suffer very much. Our infant mortality rate is among the lowest in the world, our incomes are highest, and we have nonprofits that help people who are struggling.

Our ease of life means we don't suffer much. We drive cars that compete with NASA on the amount of technology inside them. Those cars effortlessly take us where we want to go and get us there when we want to be there. Why walk when you can drive a car? We have garages to keep our vehicles warm and protected. Why spend time scraping ice off your windshield in the morning before work when you can keep it in a garage? We use dishwashers that save us time. Why spend fifteen minutes washing dishes by hand when you can spend two minutes putting them in a dishwasher? We have banks that protect our money and even give us interest on what we let them hold. Why bother to keep money in a safe at home when you can let someone pay you to hold it for you? We have washing machines and dryers so that we don't have to wash our clothes in a lake or river. Why spend hours taking our laundry to the lake to wash it and then hanging it to dry when a machine can do that for us?

These things form a worldview that looks for convenience. They train us to expect easy solutions to complex problems.

Suffering is traumatic in America because we pursue pleasure and personal freedom.[1] Because we constantly pursue pleasure and personal freedom, suffering is hard for us. That focus and pursuit shapes how we view God. I believe pastor Tim Keller is correct when he writes, "Often the unstated assumption of many people is that God's job is to create a world in which things benefit us."[2] That's why suffering is so hard for us as Americans. When our life constantly looks for easy solutions and convenience, we struggle greatly when we hit a bump in the road or a dead end. The truth is that Americans do not suffer well because Americans do not suffer very much.

Our time in the book of 1 Peter has taught us a lot about suffering. Peter has taught us about sharing the Savior in suffering (1 Pet 3:13–17). In chapter 2 we were taught to be fearful of God (vv. 13–14), to be fervent to defend God (vv. 15–16), and to be faithful to God's will (v. 17).

We've learned about the trials we experience as Christians (1 Pet 3:18–22). In chapter 3 we learned we experience unrighteous suffering just like Christ did (v. 18), we proclaim victory over those who insult, ridicule, and cause us suffering (vv. 19–20), we prepare for suffering knowing God will sustain us through the suffering he allows (v. 21), and we will experience ultimate vindication from our suffering (v. 22).

We've also learned about suffering without sin (1 Pet 4:1–6). In chapter 4 we were taught that suffering removes part of the power of sin in our lives (vv. 1–2), suffering is a result from our departure from sin (vv. 3–5), and suffering is temporarily part of the sin of this world (v. 6).

We've learned what essential actions we need in suffering in chapter 5 (1 Pet 4:7–11). Peter told us to stay grounded and use sound judgment (v. 7b), to continue loving each other (v. 8), to keep hosting others (v. 9), and to use our spiritual gifts (vv. 10–11a).

1. Keller, *Walking with God*, 22.
2. Keller, *Walking with God*, 115.

Last, in chapter 6, we learned about rejoicing in righteous suffering (1 Pet 4:12–19). This means we prepare for suffering with our minds (v. 12), rejoice in suffering with our words (v. 13), glorify God in our suffering with our actions (vv. 15–16), and trust God in suffering with our soul (vv. 17–19).

While we have only focused on seven sections of Peter's letter, the entire book is about suffering. Every chapter mentions suffering or a synonym such as *trial*, *fiery ordeal*, *testing*, *harshly treated*, etc. There are twenty synonyms for suffering in 1 Peter, which only has five chapters.

In this book Peter gives us a correct view of suffering, and in the process gives us a correct view of God. Let's conclude our time together by examining Peter's words about Satan, our struggles, and a summation. A Christian life on earth includes resisting Satan, enduring struggles that God allows, and relying on a Christian community. We'll learn that what God calls us to God gets us through.

SATAN

First Peter 5:8–9 reveals Satan's role in our suffering and could probably be its own chapter, so I'll keep it concise. "Be of sober spirit, be on the alert. Your adversary, the devil, prowls around like a roaring lion, seeking someone to devour. But resist him, firm in your faith, knowing that the same experiences of suffering are being accomplished by your brethren who are in the world" (1 Pet 4:8–9). In these two verses, Peter describes our adversary as well as the actions we need to have against that adversary.

Our Adversary

The devil is our adversary. The word for "adversary" (v. 8) here is *antidikos*, which comes from an old word for opponent in a lawsuit.[3] It has the article in front of it that points the reader to

3. Robertson, *Word Pictures*, "1 Pet 5:8"; Vincent, *Word Studies*, 669.

a well-known adversary.[4] The word "devil" (v. 8) here is *diabolos*, which means slanderer.[5] Peter's message is this: Satan is our opponent and our slanderer.

Peter uses the simile of a lion to describe Satan. A lion is normally active during the day, but when persecuted it adapts to be active at night and twilight. However, lions have limited stamina. They can run up to forty-six miles per hour but only for a short period of time. In order to get their prey they have to be close. They use trees, bushes, or long grass to hide so that they can creep up on their prey. Because of this, most of their kills occur during twilight or night. Peter uses this simile of Satan as a lion to show us that Satan doesn't show up plainly and clearly. It would be easier to battle against Satan if we always knew where he was. But Satan is subtle and sly. He uses tactics that obscure and camouflage his work. He gets under, around, and behind things, then uses them to accomplish his will. Just as Satan used the king of Tyre (Ezek 28) to accomplish evil and wickedness, Satan uses evil and wicked things in our culture today such as alcohol, drugs, or pornography to accomplish his will.

With that said, what should be our response? Peter warns us about Satan but he also provides us three ways to battle Satan.

Our Actions

Our first action in response to Satan is to be sober and respect him. Peter writes, "Be of sober spirit" (1 Pet 5:8a). This has to do with our attitude. Someone I know has spent decades working for a power company. He once told me that one of the first things the power company teaches new electricians is to respect electricity. They teach newly hired employees how much electricity it takes to kill a person and how easy it is to get electrocuted. They also explain that when someone touches something with electrical current in it that it is almost impossible for the person to let go because

4. Vincent, *Word Studies*, 669; Wallace, *Greek Grammar*, 223–24.

5. BDAG, s.v. "diabolos."

the electrical current causes muscles to tighten. In this way the new workers are taught to respect electricity. And that principle is important for us too. If we are going to do battle against Satan, Peter first wants us to have a healthy respect of Satan's power and abilities to cause us harm.

Life is not a casual walk down easy street toward heaven; life is a battlefield littered with mines that Satan has placed along our way to heaven. When we place our faith in God for salvation we know we're going to heaven, but Satan's mission is to do whatever possible to delay us, stop us, knock us off track, or prevent others from joining us. To be sober means we have a serious attitude about Satan. It means we see the world in its true condition. And that true condition is that Satan is roaming around as a lion trying to devour us.

Our second action in response to Satan is to be alert and recognize him. Peter writes, "Be on the alert. Your adversary, the devil, prowls around like a roaring lion, seeking someone to devour" (1 Pet 5:8b). This has to do with discernment. When the text says "be on the alert" it comes from the Greek word *grēgoreō* that means "to be awake" or "to arouse."[6] We have to always be on guard. It means we watch carefully and look around. This is important because Satan doesn't show up in plain sight where we can see him. He's sly, crafty, and he approaches us when we are vulnerable. Just as a lion uses long grass, bushes, or trees to sneak up on its prey, we, too, have to be aware of Satan's methods of sneaking up on us. He waits until we're under a lot of stress, then suggests we enjoy not just a drink of alcohol, but that we have two or three. He whispers, "You deserve it." He waits until we have a fight with our spouse, then he leads us to a website with porn. "You have needs," he whispers. When we're struggling with materialism he shows us rich, lavish vacations of friends on Facebook. He whispers, "You should enjoy nice things like your friends do, even if you can't afford them." We have to be alert and recognize him because he doesn't use plain tactics that are easy to identify. He's sly, crafty, and waits until we are vulnerable.

6. BDAG, s.v. "grēgoreō."

Our third action in response to Satan is to be ready to resist him. Peter writes, "But resist him, firm in your faith, knowing that the same experiences of suffering are being accomplished by your brethren who are in the world" (1 Pet 5:9). This instruction from Peter relates to our actions. To resist something means to withstand with a defensive position. We have to be ready for defense because when we accept Jesus Christ as our Savior we antagonize Satan as our enemy. This requires we maintain a strong faith based on the promises and doctrine of God's word. Warren Wiersbe writes, "The better we know God's Word, the keener our spiritual senses will be to detect Satan at work."[7] This also requires we have a strong integrated relationship with a spiritual family. This is a family that is enduring suffering together, "knowing that the same experiences of suffering are being accomplished by your brethren who are in the world" (1 Pet 5:9b). This is why our churches need small-group gatherings and potlucks. These types of fellowship events allow us to share our stories and strengthen each other as members of a spiritual family.

In 1 Pet 5:8–9 we learn the first reality of suffering, which is this: *trouble in suffering is because of Satan, not us.* We need to remember that the origin of evil, sin, wickedness, and suffering is Satan. Ezekiel 28:15 says that "unrighteousness" was found in Satan and that one-third of the angels in heaven followed him. His rebellion against God was the origin of sin. Satan is out to attack us, he has demons that follow his mandates for harm, and we live in a world full of sinful temptations that he strategically places in our midst. Trouble and suffering are because of Satan, not us.

Sometimes people suffer and there's nothing they did to cause it. Good Christians get cancer and die, loyal workers can be laid off, good wives can be abused by husbands, and innocent babies die in the wombs of expectant mothers. It is hard to see people suffer innocently. But one of our roles in suffering is to be with loved ones enduring suffering so we can remind them that they did not cause this suffering. I think it helps us get through suffering when

7. Wiersbe, *Be Hopeful*, 157.

we know it's Satan that causes some of the suffering in our lives, not us.

I think we all need reminders that suffering is part of the sinful world in which we live. Satan introduced evil into the world and now we have to live through that sin and suffering because of him.

STRUGGLES

Peter moves on from Satan to describe our struggles as Christians. "After you have suffered for a little while, the God of all grace, who called you to His eternal glory in Christ, will Himself perfect, confirm, strengthen and establish you. To Him be dominion forever and ever. Amen" (1 Pet 5:10–11).

In verse 10 Peter teaches that suffering is part of God's temporary timeline. The phrase "after you have suffered for a little while" (v. 10a) is a gentle reminder that according to God's timeline—which is an eternal timeline—our suffering on this earth is temporary. It hurts, it's hard, but it's temporary.

In verse 10 Peter also teaches that suffering is part of God's call. Peter continues, "the God of all grace, who called you." There is a sense in Scripture that God knows us and selects us to be part of his family. Other similar statements about the election of believers are revealed when Peter addressed his readers in the salutation as those "who are chosen according to the foreknowledge of God the Father" (1 Pet 1:1b–2a). When Peter tells his readers to monitor their behavior he instructs them to be "like the Holy One who called you" (1 Pet 1:15). Later he calls his readers members of "a chosen race, a royal priesthood, a holy nation" (1 Pet 2:9). In that same chapter where Peter references the suffering of his readers he tells them, "You have been called for this purpose" (1 Pet 2:21). At the end of this letter Peter gives a goodbye, referencing a greeting from his colleagues in Rome who are "chosen together with you" (1 Pet 5:13). The apostle Paul is perhaps best known for the doctrine of election,[8] but Peter appears to teach it as well. Peter teaches us that our salvation is because of God's grace (1 Pet 1:10) and that God called us before we knew him (1 Pet 1:2). Please don't miss this: The fact that God has called us assures us that we are where he wants us to be. Peter reminds us that God doesn't make mistakes, but God has us where he wants us.

In verse 10 Peter has taught that suffering is temporary, part of God's call, and that suffering is also part of his work: "Christ, will Himself perfect, confirm, strengthen and establish you." These words describe resoluteness. God is working through our struggles to produce a strength of character to grow us.

In verse 11 Peter teaches us about the sovereign Lord that is eternal: "To Him be dominion forever and ever. Amen" (1 Pet 5:11). This verse is a type of doxology or dismissal. God gives us the ability to endure the suffering that he allows us to go through. Our confidence should be in Christ, not in our flesh. The book of Proverbs tells us, "The horse is prepared for the day of battle, but victory belongs to the Lord" (Prov 21:31). Our suffering is temporary, but we will enjoy God's grace and glory forever. The apostle Paul writes, "For I consider that the sufferings of this present time are not worthy to be compared with the glory that is to be revealed to us" (Rom 8:18). Peter is teaching his readers that their suffering is temporary (1 Pet 5:10), but the Lord that is allowing them to experience that suffering is eternal (1 Pet 5:11). Because that God is eternal these believers will share in his eternal glory forever.

In 1 Pet 5:10–11 we learn a second reality of suffering, which is this: *endurance in suffering is because of God, not us*. If God allows us to experience suffering, then God will help us endure suffering. When we follow God and trust him, enduring suffering is not about how tough we are or how to come up with creative ways to get out of our suffering. Instead, we look to God, we rely on God, and we trust God to walk with us through that suffering. We trust him to take us through the situation he has placed us in. Our endurance in suffering is because of God, not our abilities.

8. See Rom 8:27–30, 38–39; 1 Cor 1:8–9; Eph 1:4–14; Phil 1:6; 1 Thess 5:23–24.

This takes the pressure off of us. We don't have to ask, "How can I get through this?" Instead we ask, "I wonder how God is going to walk with me through this?" or "I wonder how God is going to work this out?" The focus is on God, not us. The responsibility is on God, not us.

In this manner, we direct our focus from us and our situation and direct that focus to God and how he will help us. Pastor John MacArthur writes, "Christians are to live with the understanding that God's purposes realized in the future require some pain in the present. While the believer is being personally attacked by the enemy, he is being personally perfected by the Lord."[9] Just as Peter has said, "Christ, will Himself perfect, confirm, strengthen and establish you" (1 Pet 5:10c). Our endurance in suffering is because of God, not us.

SUMMATION

The final three verses of Peter's letter might have been written in his own handwriting. The apostle Paul followed a similar custom in which he would write the final part of his letters in his own handwriting (2 Thess 3:17; Gal 6:11–18). In the first century, people often used what is called an amanuensis who would write the letter on behalf of someone else. (I'll explain more about the unique roles of an amanuensis after we learn who Peter's amanuensis was.)

In verse 12 we learn about Peter's amanuensis: "Through Silvanus, our faithful brother (for so I regard him), I have written to you briefly, exhorting and testifying that this is the true grace of God. Stand firm in it!" (1 Pet 5:12). Silvanus[10] became a Christian at the church in Jerusalem, was prophetically gifted, and sent to Antioch to do ministry there (Acts 15:22, 27, 32). Silvanus traveled

9. MacArthur, *MacArthur Study Bible*, 1918.

10. The name of Peter's amanuensis is Silvanus in the NASB, but the NIV and NLT translate his name "Silas." Silvanus is the Roman latinized version of Silas, which was his Greek name. The Silvanus of 1 Peter is surely the same man named Silas in Acts. BDAG, s.v. "silouanos."

with Paul on Paul's second missionary journey. In Acts 15:40—18:5 Silvanus is mentioned eleven times and he's also mentioned in several of Paul's letters (2 Cor 1:19; 1 Thess 1:1; 2 Thess 1:1).

An amanuensis likely had one of two roles in the first century. Silvanus might have assisted Peter in writing the letter. In this role Silvanus would have been writing down the words of this letter as Peter dictated them to him. This could have been a word-for-word dictation or Silvanus might have decided which words and phrases were used. This was a common practice[11] in the first century because of the value of papyrus and low level of literacy that many people had. If Silvanus did not write down words for Peter he could have delivered the letter on behalf of Peter much like a messenger or courier would do. It is also possible that Silvanus did both roles: he wrote what Peter dictated and delivered it to the churches in Asia Minor.

While we learned about Peter's amanuensis in verse 12, next we read about Peter's companions in verse 13. "She who is in Babylon, chosen together with you, sends you greetings, and so does my son, Mark" (1 Pet 5:13). In this verse Peter reveals his church, "She who is in Babylon," which is a metaphor to describe Rome. Just as Babylon had been an enemy and persecutor of the nation of Israel, so now Rome is functioning in that same way. Peter's letter is peppered with metaphors and similes. He says we have been sprinkled with Christ's blood (1 Pet 1:2), that we should desire the milk of God's word (1 Pet 2:2), that we are being built up as living stones (1 Pet 2:4–5), that the leaders should shepherd the flock among themselves (1 Pet 5:1–4), and that Satan is like a roaring lion (1 Pet 5:8–9). It should not surprise us that Peter uses a metaphor to describe the city of Rome by using the name Babylon. With that said, this is a figurative reference to the church in Rome from where Peter was writing. In this verse Peter also reveals his calling: "chosen together with you." If God has called us to this we know he will carry us through this. In this verse Peter also reveals his coworker: "my son, Mark." The early tradition of the church

11. Tertius is the man identified in Rom 16:22 as the one who "wrote down" the words of Paul's letter to the Romans.

tells us that Mark's Gospel is based on the eye-witness testimonies of Peter.[12] This was the same Mark that failed Paul (Acts 13:13; 15:38–29; Col 4:10), but later became useful for ministry (2 Tim 4:11). Mark being in Rome with Peter makes sense because in Paul's letter to the believers in Colossae Paul says he left Mark in Rome on an earlier occasion (Col 4:10–11).

In verse 14 we see Peter's goodbye: "Greet one another with a kiss of love. Peace be to you all who are in Christ" (1 Pet 5:14). That kiss was a common sign of fellowship and Christian love (see Rom 16:16; 2 Cor 13:12; 1 Thess 5:26). Before you get too excited about kissing other people at church, you should know that early church tradition in the first couple centuries followed this practice only among the same sexes. Men only kissed men and women only kissed women. That *peace* was the same way that Peter began his letter (1 Pet 1:2) in which he told these Christians—who were in the midst of persecution and suffering—to seek the prince of peace that provides peace.

In 1 Pet 5:12–14 we learn a third reality of suffering which is this: *perseverance in suffering is easier with others.* Community is needed. Peter is in Rome but he is not alone. We need community especially in hard times. In his book *True Community*, Jerry Bridges writes, "God has created us to be dependent both on Him and on one another. . . . None of us has the spiritual wherewithal to 'go it alone' in our Christian lives. Spiritual fellowship is not a luxury but a necessity, vital to our spiritual growth and health. . . . One of the most important things we can share with one another is the spiritual truth God has been teaching us that might be of great help to fellow believers."[13] Bridges shares the correct reasons we—as the Christian church—gather together for assembly and worship. We gather together, not just to listen to a sermon or sing songs to God, but to check in on each other. We gather with each other so we can inquire how others are doing. And when someone

12. Papias (AD 60–130), Irenaeus (AD 125–202), Origen (AD 185–253), Clement of Alexandria (AD 150–215), and Jerome (AD 342–420) all taught that Mark wrote the Gospel of Mark and obtained his material from Peter.

13. Bridges, *True Community*, 60.

is not with us for an extended period of time it's good for us to call that person and ask how he is doing and see how we can minister to him.

Some people say they don't need the church; but the truth is that the people of the church need them. You have likely met people that say, "I read my Bible, I pray, and I listen to sermons online. I don't need the church." But, the people of the church need to hear other people's stories. The church needs to hear how God is speaking to them, how God is sustaining them in their suffering, and how God is working in their lives. In our church I sometimes think about what our church would be like if we did not have the powerful testimonies of the people there. I think of a man named John who is a member of our church, but for decades he used to drive his mom to church, leave her there, then return to pick her up. On potluck days he would even carry her food inside but still walk back to his car and drive home. He did not become a Christian until his mom passed away.

Sometimes I think about what our church would be like without Shirley. She spent many years addicted to drugs. It wasn't until the death of her mom and an HIV positive diagnosis that she says God grabbed her heart. The first couple times she went to church she sat in her car in the parking lot and watched the people going in and out of the church. After a few Sundays one of the ladies invited her inside.

Sometimes I think about what our church would be like without Marion. She spent the first twenty weeks of her life in the neonatal intensive care unit. She's been hospitalized many other times, has endured surgeries on her spine, and continues to fight for survival. All of this happened after doctors told Marion's pregnant mother that Marion wouldn't survive childbirth.

Perseverance in suffering is easier with others. That's why we need others to be with us sharing their stories of suffering because it helps us persevere through our trials.

Let's conclude this chapter with a quote from the late Ray Stedman, who served as senior pastor at Peninsula Bible Church in Palo Alto, California, for forty years. "This present suffering is just for a little while. Then Christ Himself will restore us to strength and health—a strength that can never fail, a vitality that can never fade, reserved for us in heaven. The world is temporal and temporary. God will bring an end to the world—*but you and I will go on forever with Him*. This is God's plan."[14]

While we might feel like things are spinning out of control, God still is in charge. When we don't know what tomorrow will be like, God still does. This is the heart of the message of 1 Peter that we have examined in this book.

I hope that 1 Peter can be a book that we go to in our times of suffering. I hope it can be a book that we use to comfort others in their suffering, whether it be a difficult marriage, a frustrating job, a wayward child, a financial burden, or a debilitating health issue.

However big or little, God has called us to faith in him, he's allowed us to be in the situation we're facing, and he will enable us to endure it.

14. Stedman, *Adventuring Through the Bible*, 820.

Epilogue

SOMETIMES WE EXPERIENCE PAIN and suffering that we do not cause. When we suffer we need to remember that our viewpoint is limited. Our limited viewpoint of pain and suffering compared to God is similar to our understanding of the shape of the earth prior to 1931.

For more than a thousand years we knew the earth was round, but we could not prove that the earth was round. We knew it *intellectually*, but we could not prove it *physically*. That was until 1931, when Captain Albert Stevens, an officer in the US Army Air Corps, took his airplane to twenty-one thousand feet above the earth and took a picture of the Andes Mountains in front of him, which are 22,838 feet above the earth. If the earth was flat the Andes Mountains should have been level or slightly above the horizon of his picture, which he took from 287 miles away. But the Andes Mountains were well below the horizon of his picture, thus serving as the first physical evidence that the earth was round.[1] For years we *knew* intellectually that the earth was round, but we couldn't prove it or *see* it physically.

And that's sometimes how it works for us when we as Christians are in pain and suffering. We *know* that God is good, loves us, and has a plan. But it's hard to endure pain and suffering because we can't *see* his plan. We can't see the whole picture that God is painting.

1. Uri, "90 Years of Views," paras. 3–4.

If there's one thing we've learned from our study of 1 Peter it's that *we rely on God to get us through difficult circumstances.* Christians are not exempt from difficulties and troubles. Being a Christian does not prevent heartache, disappointment, and sadness.

When nothing makes sense and when everything falls apart, that's when we trust God and look to God to get us through it all. As pastor Mark Hitchcock has said, "The bigger God is to us, the smaller our troubles will seem. And the smaller God is, the larger our troubles will seem."[2] At some point we need to take our eyes off our difficulties and look to God because God is the only one that can help us get through tough experiences.

With God we can endure difficulties and trials because he sustains us. He'll walk with us through our troubles, help us endure temptation, make a way for us to live with a disability, and show us how to endure poor times. He did that for Peter and Peter's readers, and I know he will do that for you and me too.

2. Hitchcock, "How Big Is God?"

Bibliography

Bramer, Stephen. *The Bible Reader's Joke Book*. Self-published, 2014.

Bridges, Jerry. *True Community: The Biblical Practice of Koinonia*. Carol Stream, IL: NavPress, 2012.

Constable, Thomas. *Notes on 1 Peter*. 2025 ed. Sonic Light, 2023. https://soniclight.com/tcon/notes/pdf/1peter.pdf.

Evans, Tony. *The Tony Evans Bible Commentary: Advancing God's Kingdom Agenda*. Nashville: Holman, 2019.

Hitchcock, Mark. "How Big Is Your God?" Faith Bible Church, August 28, 2016. https://faithbibleok.subspla.sh/rnz6q2q.

Jones, Martin Lloyd. *Spiritual Depression: Its Causes and Cure*. Grand Rapids: Eerdmans, 1965.

Keener, Craig. *1 Peter: A Commentary*. Grand Rapids: Baker Academic, 2021.

Keller, Tim. *Walking with God Through Pain and Suffering*. New York: Penguin, 2015.

MacArthur, John, ed. *MacArthur Study Bible, New American Standard Bible*. Nashville: Thomas Nelson, 2006.

McGee, J. Vernon. *1 Peter*. Thru the Bible Commentary Series 54. Nashville: Thomas Nelson, 1991.

McVean, Ada. "Broken Bones Grow Back Stronger . . . Sort Of." McGill Office for Science and Society, April 19, 2018. https://www.mcgill.ca/oss/article/did-you-know/broken-bones-grow-back-stronger-sort.

Merriam-Webster. *Merriam-Webster's Collegiate Dictionary*. 11th ed. Springfield, MA: Merriam-Webster, 2003.

Missionary Church. "International Day of Prayer for the Persecuted Church." https://mcusa.org/news/idop2023.

Morgan, Robert J. *Preacher's Sourcebook of Creative Sermon Illustrations*. Nashville: Thomas Nelson, 2007.

Mounce, William B. *Basics of Biblical Greek Grammar*. 3rd ed. Grand Rapids: Zondervan, 2009.

Open Doors. "The 2025 World Watch List." https://www.opendoorsus.org/en-US/persecution/countries/.

Osborne, Grant R. "1 Peter." In *James, 1 & 2 Peter, Jude, Revelation*, edited by Philip W. Comfort, 129–272. Cornerstone Biblical Commentary 20. Carol Stream, IL: Tyndale House, 2011.

Pettegree, Andrew, and Arthur der Weduwen. *The Library: A Fragile History*. New York: Basic, 2021.

Raymer, Roger M. "1 Peter." In *The Bible Knowledge Commentary: New Testament*, edited by John F. Walvoord and Roy B. Zuck, 837–58. Colorado Springs: Cook, 1983.

Robertson, Archibald T. *Word Pictures in the New Testament*. Nashville: Broadman, 1933. Logos.

Ryrie, Charles. *Ryrie Study Bible, New American Standard Version*. Chicago: Moody, 1985.

———. *A Survey of Bible Doctrine*. Chicago: Moody, 1972.

Schnabel, Eckhard J. "The Persecution of Christians in the First Century." *Journal of the Evangelical Theological Society* 61 (2018) 525–47.

Scott, Christopher L. "Suffering in 1 Peter." Christopher L. Scott, September 26, 2025. https://christopherlynnscott.com/suffering-in-1-peter/.

Sproul, R. C. *1–2 Peter: An Expositional Commentary*. Samford, FL: Ligonier Ministries, 2019.

Stedman, Ray C. *Adventuring Through the Bible: A Comprehensive Guide to the Entire Bible*. Grand Rapids: Discovery House, 2012.

Swindoll, Charles. *Insights on James, 1 & 2 Peter*. Swindoll's Living Insights New Testament Commentary 13. Carol Stream, IL: Tyndale House, 2014.

Tacitus. *Complete Works of Tacitus*. Edited by Moses Hadas, translated by Alfred John Church and William Jackson Brodribb. The Modern Library. New York: Random House, 1942.

Tada, Joni Eareckson. *Her Story: The Three Bestselling Autobiographies Complete In One Volume*. New York: Inspiration, 1994.

Toussaint, Stanley. "Subjection: The Duty of the Believer; 1 Pet. 2:11—3:12." Lecture 4, section 8 of *BE107: Hebrews, General Epistles and Revelation*. Dallas Theological Seminary. https://media.dts.edu/player/?course=BE107&unit=4&video=8&language=en-US.

Tripp, Paul David. *Suffering: Gospel Hope When Life Doesn't Make Sense*. Wheaton, IL: Crossway, 2018.

Uri, John. "90 Years of Our Changing Views of Earth." NASA, December 21, 2020. https://www.nasa.gov/feature/90-years-of-our-changing-views-of-earth.

Vincent, Marvin Richardson. *Word Studies in the New Testament*. New York: Scribner's Sons, 1887. Logos.

Wallace, Daniel B. *Greek Grammar Beyond the Basics: An Exegetical Syntax of the New Testament with Scripture, Subject, and Greek Word Indexes*. Grand Rapids: Zondervan, 1997.

Walls, David, and Max Anders. *I & II Peter, I, II & III John, Jude*. Holman New Testament Commentary 11. Nashville: Broadman & Holman, 1999. Logos.

Walvoord, John F. *Every Prophecy of the Bible: Clear Explanations for Uncertain Times by One of Today's Premier Prophecy Scholars*. Colorado Springs: Chariot Victor, 1999.

Wiersbe, Warren W. *Be Hopeful (1 Peter): How to Make the Best of Times Out of Your Worst of Times*. 2nd ed. Colorado Springs: Cook, 2009.

———. *The Bumps Are What You Climb On: Encouragement for Difficult Days*. Grand Rapids: Baker, 2002.

Zemeckis, Robert, dir. *Back to the Future*. Amblin Entertainment and Universal Pictures, 1985.

www.ingramcontent.com/pod-product-compliance
Lightning Source LLC
LaVergne TN
LVHW020652100826
845148LV00012B/2452